T0304756

Process Downtime Reduction

Among the biggest mistakes manufacturers make is not keeping key equipment and processes running and making saleable product when needed. This situation existed when the author Mike Beauregard began working in manufacturing years ago and it currently remains true in companies ostensibly focusing on Lean. To improve, companies often rely on increasing productivity by making products faster and with more automation, but many fail to focus on the area in which they can get the biggest gains for their efforts – the reduction of downtime.

This book provides readers the techniques they crucially need to keep their critical manufacturing equipment running correctly and efficiently – which increases production, decreases labor costs, decreases breakdown costs, and ultimately increases the bottom line.

Downtime in production lines stems from many sources. The contribution might be small for many of those sources, but it adds up. Downtime and its causes then insidiously become the norm, accepted, unseen by the workforce and the management team. Most training courses and books look at a specific cause of downtime – mainly, either product changeover (set-up reduction) or breakdowns (TPM). This book addresses these two areas and many other sources of downtime including how to decrease downtime caused by supply chain issues, staffing issues, and downtime internal to the processes themselves.

In the final chapter, the author covers how to manage the downtime reduction effort – how to measure downtime, prioritize which downtime sources to attack first, and monitor the improvement.

Process Downtime Reduction

How to Minimize Waste from Breakdowns, Set-Ups, Supply Chain Issues, and Staffing Constraints

Michael R. Beauregard

Routledge
Taylor & Francis Group

A PRODUCTIVITY PRESS BOOK

First published 2024
by Routledge
605 Third Avenue, New York, NY 10158

and by Routledge
4 Park Square, Milton Park, Abingdon, Oxon, OX14 4RN

Routledge is an imprint of the Taylor & Francis Group, an informa business

© 2024 Michael R. Beauregard

The right of Michael R. Beauregard to be identified as author of this work has been asserted by him in accordance with sections 77 and 78 of the Copyright, Designs and Patents Act 1988.

ISBN: 9781032445496 (hbk)
ISBN: 9781032445489 (pbk)
ISBN: 9781003372714 (ebk)

DOI: 10.4324/9781003372714

Typeset in Garamond
by Deanta Global Publishing Services, Chennai, India

To Maura, who constantly strives for no downtime in life.

Contents

List of Figures

Foreword

As the vice president of manufacturing for a rapidly growing company, I am always striving to improve our operations, to better serve our customers. I constantly battle downtime.

Almost 10 years ago, when we had just one site, I brought in Mike Beauregard as a manufacturing consultant to help our improvement efforts. Today, with four sites in our portfolio and with our growth still strong, we have over a dozen successful projects under our belt with Mike. We have worked together on productivity improvement, set-up reduction efforts, and plant workflow and layout projects. These projects have now covered all four of our manufacturing facilities. For when I face tough manufacturing issues, I have Mike on speed-dial. He has become an integral part of helping guide our business processes and manufacturing improvement efforts.

Mike gave me a draft of *Process Downtime Reduction* and asked for my input and endorsement. I had no time to spare, but I felt it was essential to anyone trying to grow their manufacturing to read *Process Downtime Reduction*. My endorsement expanded into this Foreword.

I knew of Mike's time living in Japan and studying the Toyota Production System while working at one of the Toyota keiretsu companies there. I knew he spent some time learning from Ohno. He shared some of that learned knowledge with my staff and me during our projects. In *Process Downtime Reduction*, he shares that knowledge and more. While reading the draft, I could hear him in my head "Anytime your fillers are down and not dispensing into bottles, you're not making any money." It got old, but he correctly kept our focus there.

I recognized many of the techniques discussed in the book. Many are common sense manufacturing. Some are areas we worked on with Mike. And some are tribal knowledge that Mike has picked up in his years in the manufacturing trenches. *Process Downtime Reduction* is Mike documenting a portion of that tribal knowledge and passing it down.

Over the years, Mike helped our plants, but more importantly he helped me develop the skills of my manufacturing and engineering staffs by continually sharing his knowledge and experience. I highly recommend you read *Process Downtime Reduction* to develop your skills further. Then use the book to build the skills of your manufacturing and engineering staff by having them read it and apply its contents to your operation. This will reap dividends for you and your business.

Brian King

Preface

I have worked in manufacturing for a while now. I visit dozens of companies a year. Many things have changed in manufacturing over the years, but one thing remains constant – too many processes and pieces of equipment sit idle too much of the time. I observe that in nearly every manufacturing facility I visit. And that never sits well with me, especially when on the plant tour, I see the KPIs on the wall showing On-Time Delivery never reaching 100% and the product Lead Time graph trending upwards.

Invariably I am told there are legitimate reasons (pronounced "ex-cus-es") for the equipment or processes being down. Look at the number of supply chain issues we face today. We cannot find workers willing to work in manufacturing. Plus our equipment is aging and breaking down on us. Or our customers keep changing their orders, pulling them in/pushing them out and changing quantities. And those are just the most common of the litany of excuses I hear on my tours.

I have heard these reasons for downtime almost a mile into the earth where a nickel miner sat idle waiting for his drilling machine to be repaired. I have heard them in aerospace companies, automotive companies, medical device companies – any type of manufacturing you can imagine. And I have heard them at process equipment companies, including at one where 12 of 14 assembly stations sat with partially assembled, million-dollar-plus machines not being worked on. Management there had brought me in under the pretense of needing consulting help, but only wanted me to validate to their bosses that they were approaching manufacturing the "right way." No validity there.

Sorry, but I cannot buy into many of the reasons I'm given for downtime as valid.

Much of the issue is that we never take the time to think of downtime systematically. We address it piecemeal – we have set-up reduction efforts where we train key folks in set-up reduction techniques. Then we move on to our maintenance approach and have teams working on TPM efforts. On to 5Ss (or 6). We have supply chain efforts – which we do not need Manufacturing to participate in, right? We have many individual efforts – "flavor of the month" some call it – but we fail to look at the entire picture.

My decision to put this book together came while I was preparing for a talk on downtime reduction for a quality conference. As I copied slides out of my set-up reduction workshop, problem-solving workshop, and several other presentations and leafed through four or five separate reference books to cull out material for the talk, I felt there was a need for one go-to on downtime reduction on my shelf. Not finding a book I liked, I decided to author one using the knowledge I've gained, mostly the hard way, working in manufacturing over the years.

In putting this book together, I'd like to thank a few people for their help – Frank Gillern, one of the most common sense manufacturing experts out there, for his excellent input, Ashish Gulanikar, Jim Fusco, and Lou Cassone for their supply chain expertise, my endorsers Chiaki Umeno, Bob Fox, and Brian King for their suggestions after reviewing the first draft, Alan Houghton for his financial insight, and the editorial staff at Deanta for making sense of my conversational style.

May this work help your processes live long and prosper!

Mike

About the Author

Michael R. Beauregard is a manufacturing, engineering, and quality professional. He consults and trains companies worldwide in the application of lean and quality improvement techniques to positively impact their operations. Mike is an eight-time member of the Board of Examiners for the Malcolm Baldrige National Quality Award. He is certified in lean implementation by the Supplier Excellence Alliance (SEA), the aerospace supply-chain consortium. He is a CT-registered Professional Engineer and an ASQ-Certified Quality Engineer.

Chapter 1

Introduction: "Your Order Is Going to Be Late"

As a manufacturing professional, there is nothing worse than calling up your sales force to tell them that the order for their largest customer, that critical order for them, is going to be late. Well, almost nothing worse – you could have to call the customer yourself that the order is delayed!

Regardless of whether it's the sales force or the customer you have to tell, the recipient of the bad news is not going to be happy. And they are going to want to know when you can ship the order out. How do you tell them that your key machine just had to be shipped out for repairs, or that you can't afford to break into an extended run for another large customer because you can't afford the cost of the downtime needed to change over all the equipment in the process to make their product?

All too often, we cannot meet our manufacturing commitments because of process downtime – our process just sitting there churning out nothing – when we need that process to be producing to fill that order and keep it from being late.

Process downtime is ugly. There are no two ways to describe it. It is like navigating a ship through a reef shrouded in fog (Figure 1.1). We have to operate in special ways because of the fog of downtime and we never know when we are going to pile up on the reef with its protrusions. The fog allows little warning that we are in danger. Our business could sink on late shipments and the resulting lost customers, high inventory levels and little manufacturing flexibility, poor employee morale, and perhaps most

DOI: 10.4324/9781003372714-1

Figure 1.1 The fog of downtime

importantly, lost revenue. Money that our business needs to keep healthy and be positioned for success.

Downtime = Lost $$

When thinking about downtime, most people mentally jump immediately to money and specifically to their labor costs. The cost of an operator sitting idle while Maintenance repairs the process equipment. The cost of an operator performing non-value-added tasks with the line down, such as you have during a product changeover. This transforms into the thought that if you cut downtime, you will reduce the amount and cost of labor needed to perform the work to make parts or products.

This is true. Cutting downtime can reduce labor costs, reduce the costs of your products, and put the company in better shape financially. But labor savings is not the big number in the money equation. There can be much larger financial gains achieved if the time saved by reducing downtime can be converted to making products that you subsequently sell – here you gain the entire manufacturing contribution less taxes for the additional product made. Additional manufacturing contribution normally impacts financial performance and health much greater than labor savings does. [Note here that the big assumption is that your sales force actually sells the additional production you picked up by reducing downtime.]

If your company operates profitably or at breakeven, you are already covering your fixed costs (overhead) with the products currently being made and sold. Any additional product made during saved downtime and sold does not need to carry any overhead burden. Your only costs for that additional product are the variable costs associated with it – costs such as direct labor fully loaded to include benefit expenses, raw material costs including consumable supplies, packaging costs, and shipping costs. For any product made during the time saved, you pick up the entire manufacturing contribution from that product before taxes – the net sales price minus the variable costs.

Cutting Prices

Instead of flowing the additional manufacturing contribution from downtime reduction to the bottom line, some organizations look to lower their pricing in an attempt to gain more market share. The financial calculations to determine how far you can lower prices are complex and beyond the scope of this book. The advantage cutting prices gains you in the marketplace can be debatable. But be very careful in the calculations. Remember that the additional manufacturing contribution stems only from the additional product made during what was downtime. Price cuts apply to all the product sold. You probably cannot decrease prices as much as you initially think you can. And if you ever have to pull a price cut back from customers, well, good luck with that.

A Midwest stamping operation that supplies parts to a military contractor had an opportunity to supply three stock keeping units (SKUs) for a high-volume weapons system. The press they needed to stamp the parts had no capacity remaining – but it did have an average of 1266 minutes per week of downtime just for product changeovers, switching the press over from one part to another. By improving the set-up process, we were able to reduce the downtime for product changeovers to 36 minutes, which picked up 175 minutes per changeover, or 1050 minutes per week. We could stamp parts for 1050 more minutes per week.

The press had a 1.2-second cycle time for the new parts so each week the operation could produce 52,500 more parts during the downtime saved.

Manufacturing Contribution per Part

= Net Sales Price-Direct Labor-Material Costs-Packaging-Shipping

= $0.25 per part

Annual Parts Made During Former Downtime

$$= \frac{1050\,min}{week} \times \frac{50\,weeks}{year} \times \frac{60\,sec}{min} \times \frac{1\,part}{1.2\,sec}$$

= 2,625,000 parts per year

Annual Manufacturing Contribution

$$= \frac{2,625,000\,parts}{year} \times \frac{\$0.25}{part}$$

= $656,250 per year

Figure 1.2 Manufacturing contribution calculation

With an average manufacturing contribution across the three SKUs of 25¢ per part, the company annually gained over $656,000 less taxes flowing to the bottom line from the sale of these parts (Figure 1.2).

By comparison, if you just looked at labor costs, for the hours saved by reducing the downtime, they still would have saved over $54,000 per year at a labor rate of $62/hour fully loaded. Nothing to sneeze about, but still an order of magnitude lower than the money produced by the manufacturing contribution from the parts being made and sold.

Labor Savings

The big issue on labor savings is whether they are real or not. All too often labor savings are just paper calculations. They are not realized savings.

At a dinner for the Board of Examiners of the Malcolm Baldrige National Quality Award, I sat next to the commander of one of the U.S. Navy's aviation repair facilities. He told our table the story of how when he took over the facility, he reviewed a 15-inch stack of reports from improvement teams.

The results amazed him. They amazed him to the point where he went back to the top of the stack and started aggregating the cost and labor savings in a spreadsheet. He told us that when he finished the stack, his numbers showed that each repaired aircraft "was returned to the fleet before it even got there [to the repair facility] and returned with a bag of money in it." The total labor time saved by the improvement teams according to the reports exceeded the actual time it took to repair the aircraft and the total costs saved exceeded the cost of the repairs made.

The commander received a lot of laughs from his story, but the story underscores the problem with calculating labor savings. The only time that labor savings are truly real is when overtime is cut, temporary labor is reduced or eliminated, someone leaves and the position is not filled, or someone gets laid off. The last of these should not be your option unless you have bleeding approaching fatality levels.

Manufacturing contribution is the way to go to calculate the financial benefits of downtime reduction to your company.

Other Costs of Process Downtime

The ugliness of downtime doesn't just translate into unhappy customers and lost contribution. Process downtime can cost your organization in many ways. Here are just some of the other real costs of process downtime.

A Lost Customer

People in general are very forgiving. Even business people. They almost always will give your organization a second chance (there are some exceptions to this, such as when an executive I once worked for wrecked a customer's Ferrari…). But third and fourth chances are rarer. And downtime can use up your "9 lives" quickly. If a process is repeatedly down, this will invariably cause late shipments. Most companies are keeping inventory levels very tight these days. A late shipment will affect their schedule and plans. So enough late shipments and the customer will have to move in a new direction. They will have to find a more reliable supplier.

Need for High Inventory Levels

You might try to beat the downtime problem by carrying high inventory levels. This way you can supply even when the process is down. A good buffer of safety stock will save the day, right? Not if you start tying up too much cash in inventory. Cash flow is the lifeblood of any operation so needlessly tying up cash is like cutting off the blood flow to the business.

Holding inventory is like taking your wallet and putting it up on an inaccessible shelf. Yes, that money in the wallet is yours, but you can't use it for anything. You can't get the milk your wife asked you to bring home or buy that lottery ticket that will change your life. You can't do anything with the money in that wallet – you have to obtain more money another way to make the purchases you need.

And with high inventory levels, there also lies the risk of obsolescence. Companies are making design changes to improve and reduce the costs of their products more rapidly than ever. If you keep high inventory levels, you run the risk of just having to throw it out or sell it as scrap. At one plastics molder that specializes in condiment squeeze-bottle caps, I saw them grinding up 3.5 million mustard caps because their customer made a minor cosmetic change to the design.

Need for Long Runs

Your schedule can be full of long production runs if you experience high levels of process downtime for breakdowns and for product changeovers. If the process is running, you'd better not shut it down just in case it breaks and you can't get it back up and running quickly. Or if it takes hours or days to change over a process to the next product, then you need to have long runs to amortize the costs of that long changeover into the per-piece price. You end up making a product that is just going to get placed in a storage rack somewhere, not a product that you can immediately sell, or you set your minimum order quantities (MOQ) high and force your customers to take more parts than they want or need. The former impacts your cash flow and inventory costs, and the latter impacts your relationship with your customer. One of my cosmetics customers dropped one of their main contract fillers and switched to a higher-priced contract filler because the original supplier insisted on 5000-piece MOQs and the new supplier offered a 1000-piece minimum.

Less Flexibility in Responding to Customers' Changing Needs

In an effort to drive down their costs, many manufacturers are cutting their inventory levels and even the size of orders they place with their suppliers. This means that if their demand changes, they need quick reaction from their supply base. If their order increases, high inventory levels might protect you from this. Of course, it will only protect you if you have the right thing in stock. There have been many companies burned badly these last few years with supply chain issues.

In all likelihood, you've been trying to reduce your inventory levels. Without the ability to get their product up and running in your operation quickly, you might find that the customer goes elsewhere to get the stock because you don't have the flexibility in your operations to meet rapid changes in their needs. If they find the product elsewhere once, what is to keep them from moving to the other source permanently?

Higher Costs

Process downtime also leads to higher costs not just in labor – costs for materials or components lost in start-up and shut-down of a machine; energy costs for process equipment like ovens that can't be shut down for short periods while repairs are made on other parts of the process; maintenance costs for emergency repairs; and even costs for those high-priced consultants who are going to tell you how to do it the "right" way. There can be higher costs from downtime in every part of the operation.

Poor Employee Morale

This one often isn't as clear as the others, but process downtime can also have big impacts on employee morale. No one likes to work on a process that is always breaking down (and this is obviously even worse if the breakdown could potentially affect employee safety). And very few people like to be idle, waiting for their process to be back up and running.

These days most workers know the impact that their operations have on a company. They know that if they aren't producing, their jobs are in jeopardy. The more process downtime they see and experience, the greater the jeopardy to the whole company. This fear can greatly affect morale.

This can become a death spiral (Figure 1.3) because as downtime goes up, employee morale drops more. As morale drops, employees start to leave. And who leaves first? – your better employees; those that are motivated by

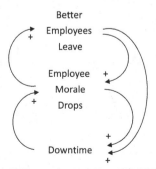

Figure 1.3   Causal loop of downtime's impact on employee morale and retention

change and those with the best, most marketable skills. As they leave, this further impacts morale as well as downtime itself directly. The loops reinforce themselves downward.

Poorer Competitive Position

All of the issues above result in your company stuck in a poorer competitive position. All because of downtime. Reducing downtime can only improve your competitive position – cutting costs, increasing margins, and keeping customers happy. And think of the potential you have to gain market share if you can cut your prices while maintaining a high-quality product!

We've seen the pain that downtime can cause, let's look at some of the sources of downtime.

Process Downtime

They say it pretty well in metals machining – "If you aren't cutting chips, you aren't making money!" When your process sits idle, it is adding no value. No matter what you are making or what type of process you have, if it is down, it is just costing you.

The reasons why a process might go down stem from problems and interactions among the thousands of variables in any process. These variables can be broadly categorized into People, Materials, Equipment, Methods, Environment, and Measurement System – aka Shewhart's Concept of a Process (Figure 1.4). These variables, the causes, create the output, the effect. When a process runs well, it outputs saleable product.

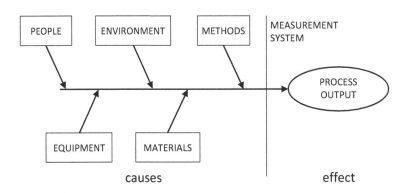

Figure 1.4   Shewhart's concept of a process

But the "output" of the process can also be process downtime. We can organize causes of downtime similarly as shown in Figure 1.5.

Most companies have downtime arising from many of these, although the one which contributes most to total downtime varies from company to company. Product changeovers and equipment breakdowns are the most obvious to most manufacturing professionals, but I've seen companies where personnel issues are No. 1 on the Pareto hit parade. And at one cosmetics contract manufacturer, it was material that caused more than half their downtime – the bottles, jars, and components that they filled with cosmetics were provided by their customers and frequently were late or rejected by Quality at incoming inspection. Let's look at some of these causes:

- Inefficiencies in changing over from one product to the next
- Equipment breakdowns
- Personnel issues
- Scheduling issues
- Material unavailability
- Process cycle inefficiencies

Product Changeovers

Product changeover downtime occurs when the process is down as one product is being cleared, the process cleaned out, and then converted to manufacture another product. The best companies in the world take minutes to do this. Other companies can take days. If you take minutes, then

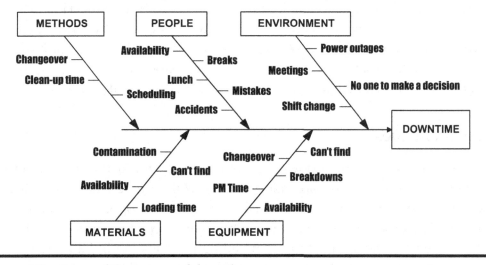

Figure 1.5   Some of the causes of downtime

this isn't an issue for you. If it is taking days, then it costs you dearly. At one plastic bottle manufacturer I worked with, a changeover took them 34 hours. Not only did they have to amortize the costs for those 34 hours into the bottle cost but they also lost the manufacturing contribution from the bottles that could have been made in that time period. When we cut that time down to just over 4 hours, they picked up nearly 30 hours of production each changeover. They could produce more, and the shorter bottle campaigns this allowed resulted in a decrease in finished goods inventories.

Equipment Breakdowns

This is pretty self-explanatory. Nothing is being produced while a line is down for repairs. Most downtime for equipment breakdown occurs for emergency repairs because companies fail to take care of their equipment on a regular basis. They are surprised and not ready when it fails. They don't have the people, parts, and sometimes even the techniques in place to make those repairs. There is a scramble to call workers in, to find or make parts, and in some cases to find a contractor who can come in right now to make the repairs.

Even companies that schedule repairs because their equipment is broken, but operable, can have excessive downtime for the repairs. Often little thought is given to minimizing the downtime associated with a planned repair. While planned repairs normally take less time than emergency repairs, they often take more time than they really need.

The best companies use preventive and predictive maintenance techniques to prevent process breakdowns and unexpected repairs. This is time well spent. But preventive maintenance is often done with the equipment down, i.e., downtime. Companies need to look at how they can minimize the downtime associated with preventive maintenance while ensuring they perform the maintenance activities needed to prevent breakdowns.

Personnel Issues

I've seen critical equipment down for hours per day for lack of personnel to run them. A key broaching operation at an aircraft engine facility was often down for 4 hours per day because there was only one operator trained to run it. She was a long-term employee who had 5 weeks of vacation. She really helped out the company by scheduling her vacation in half-day increments. Parts piled up in the cell in front of the broach when she was out.

No one else was trained to run that broach. No surprise that the department was invariably behind in orders and working overtime to catch up.

Then there are breaks, lunch, and shift change. While some industries such as the chemical process industry run their equipment through breaks, lunch, and shift change, many others do not. They don't even run bottleneck equipment during those times. At many sites, a 15-minute morning break, 30-minute lunch, 15-minute afternoon break, and shift change keep the equipment down for 1 to 2 hours per shift. And heaven help the operation that is located across the plant from the break room because their downtime is even more – the operators need to get ready to go to break, don't they? And then they have travel time to and from break. Wouldn't want to leave the break room before the horn sounds that the break is over!

When I first took over managing a component manufacturing plant, the operators shut down at 3 pm for a 4 pm shift change – they had to clean up and get ready to go home. Then when the second shift came in, that crew had to get ready to run. Most of the plant operations didn't start up until 4:20 or later. Multiply this by three shifts per day and we had 4 hours of downtime just for shift change. It took a year to change that culture and my team and I certainly did not win many friends on the shop floor converting most of that time to productive work.

Scheduling Issues

The production schedule and last-minute changes to the schedule also create process downtime. I've seen planners schedule lines to run when they didn't have raw materials available to run in the process and other times when they didn't have operators available. And how a planner schedules the process can directly contribute to downtime – at a plastics compounding operation where I worked, the scheduler ran colors randomly so there was extensive clean-up time between each color. We went to a schedule of light colors to dark colors. This approach minimized clean-up time between each color up until the end of the run. After black was run, then a complete clean-up was done. For the minor color changes, only a minor clean-up was done – saving up to 7 hours of downtime between colors.

Material Unavailability

Companies are keeping raw material inventory levels low. If you want to keep your costs down and your cash flow up, that makes sense to do. But pulling this off successfully means that you must have selected and part-nered with good suppliers – suppliers that deliver what you need, in the quantities that you need, when you need it, and with good quality (the old Just-in-Time adage). Late shipments can mean your key process goes down while waiting on materials to arrive or while making a last-minute change-over to run a product that you have raw material for.

Some facilities will have downtime even though they have the raw mate-rial on hand just because the raw material is not out on the production line when it needs to be. This sometimes occurs simply because a material han-dler hasn't gotten the raw material out there yet. Other times it is because the raw material cannot be found in the warehouse.

Process Inefficiencies

Even while technically the process is running, there could be downtime in the cycles. Loading and unloading parts into a CNC is one example. Loading a new coil for a stamping line is another. The longer the unloading/loading cycle takes, the more lost production you have even if the operator is offi-cially clocked in as running that machine or process.

And there can be "downtime" even in processes while they are running – inefficient tooling paths, stop points in programs, and overadjustments to the process where you have to wait until it gets back to steady state.

In-process quality checks can also lead to equipment downtime. It is great that the operators are responsible for the quality and make their own quality checks, but this can lead to them walking away with the process down to make the quality check. And even if the operators don't run the quality checks themselves, some companies maintain a policy that keeps the process down until the quality department checks samples and gives them two thumbs up.

Other Sources

If you have kept track of all the potential sources or downtime touched on in this chapter, you have an extensive list already. But there are many more potential sources, with some being specific to your company and your site. Some people just call them "glitches." And when these come up for the first time, you will just shake your head when you see the process down because of them. But recognize that you need to take action on them to prevent recurrences.

The Course to Zero Downtime

Downtime is often baked into operating standards and an organization's culture. We accept it because it has been there forever. We have built it into the way things are done. We must change that mentality, clear up the fog of downtime, and stay off the reef.

No process is going to be completely free of downtime. There is always some. Even the best processes rarely average more than 95% uptime. That doesn't mean you have to settle for downtime. Like a company's safety targets, the goal is always zero. Zero accidents. Zero downtime. You might never reach that level, but that is always the goal to strive for!

And as you reduce downtime, your costs drop and your competitive edge improves.

The next chapters of this book will look at these sources of downtime we talked about here and offer ideas on how to eliminate or minimize the downtime associated with those sources. I will end with a chapter on how to begin and then manage your downtime reduction efforts.

Chapter 2

Process Set-Up Reduction

It is rare these days that a process makes only one product without any changes. Most lines make a variety of products. This means the lines need to be changed over from one product to another. The time taken to change over a process from one product to another is called the set-up, or process changeover, time. In actual measurement, this is the time from the last saleable piece of one product to the first saleable piece of the product being changed to. [I use the word "saleable" here on purpose. Some people like to state this as the last good piece to the first good piece. They stop recording their set-up time when the first good piece comes off the line and then they stop the line to march parts down for Quality checks. To me, until the process is truly running, it remains down for the set-up. I'll talk more about Quality checks as we get into this section.]

The folks at Toyota, since the days of Shingo and Ohno, have focused on set-up time and reducing it. When touring the fender stamping operation at one of their plants in Japan, I watched a changeover on a 600-ton stamping press that took less than 4 minutes according to my trusty Hamilton chronograph. That included changing out the stamping die and the material. On a line making hose connectors for under-the-hood applications, I witnessed a changeover that took less than a minute. And neither of these were automated changeovers (a lot of engineers love to throw automation at reducing changeover times, and while this might be the best way, in many cases it is not).

Both of these changeover times were within the target at Toyota for Single Minute Exchange of Die, or SMED for short. The goal at Toyota is to

DOI: 10.4324/9781003372714-2

minimize the set-up time, but at worst to have it less than 10 minutes, i.e., down in the single digits, or single minutes.

Now compare that with most companies. If you do, isn't it amazing how many companies have changeovers that take half of a shift or a whole shift or a day? I cannot tell you how many organizations I have been in where the changeovers are started in the morning and done by lunch or finished just at the end of the shift. How many companies have "even" changeover times and how many are at 4 hours, 8 hours, 16 hours, and 24 hours – two orders of magnitude greater than Toyota's target of single minutes?

So how do companies that excel at product changeovers do it? They do it just like the pit crews on racing teams. [I know everyone uses this example, but it is a great one so I'll use it too.]

Pit Stop

Think about the last time you changed a tire. How long did it take you? The last time I changed a tire, it took me 25 minutes. I was coming out of church with my two children and the woman next to me had a flat on her van. It's one of those situations where you just want to go home, but know you have to help! First, I had to find the hidden mini jack. And being a van, I had to find the hidden mechanism buried under the rear carpet that lowers the spare from under the vehicle. I had to spin the mechanism 8 gazillion times to lower the spare to the point I could free it. Later I found myself jumping on the lug wrench to break the lug nuts on the wheel free. I changed the tire and then had to finish the job by spinning the spare mechanism 8 gazillion more times to raise it up out of the way and by figuring out the jigsaw puzzle on how to stow the jack. A solid 25-minute effort.

If a racing team (Figure 2.1) took 25 minutes to change a tire, they'd be laughed off the track. They take seconds to change a tire. In fact, they take seconds to change four tires, fill the fuel tank, and get the driver a drink of water! What's different about how they do it? Loads!

1. They have the right equipment at the right place at the right time.
2. They know when the pit stop is coming so they are prepared for it.
3. They each have roles and have practiced their roles.
4. Everything is in its place. Nothing needs to be searched for.
5. Equipment is fast acting – one pump of the jack to lift the car.

Figure 2.1 Pit stop. *Drawing courtesy of Maura McGuire*

Without all of these things, the pit crew could not change a tire in just seconds! The racing team would have no chance at the checkered flag no matter how good their driver was. But think how few companies look at their changeovers in these same terms. Until they do, they will not be producing when they could be and they won't be achieving any checkered flag either.

Basic Concepts

To get started on Set-Up Reduction, let's look at some basic concepts.

Internal Time versus External Time

Set-up time can be thought of as time internal to the set-up – the time when the equipment is down, and external to the set-up – time spent on the set-up while the process is running saleable product. The preparation by the pit crew was external set-up time. It was being done while the car was still racing. The internal time for the pit crew was the time the car was off the track and in the pit.

Goals of Set-Up Reduction

There are three goals to set-up reduction:

1. Combine or eliminate set-up activities.
2. Eliminate set-up waste.
3. Convert activities being done internal to the set-up to external.

We start our set-up reduction activities by looking for steps in the set-up that can be eliminated. Then whatever cannot be eliminated, we look to see if they can be combined with another step or steps.

Setting up for production is a process and just like in any process, we want to make it Lean by eliminating its wastes – the Toyota seven wastes of waiting, transportation, processing itself, motion, poor "quality," inventory, and overproduction. In reality, we are looking at the first five of these. The wastes of inventory and overproduction are really caused by excessive set-up times.

Eliminating activities and waste will cut the downtime and the internal set-up time as shown by the bottom arrow in Figure 2.2. Then we work on the remaining activities to see which we can do before the line goes down for the set-up and which can be done after the internal set-up activities are complete.

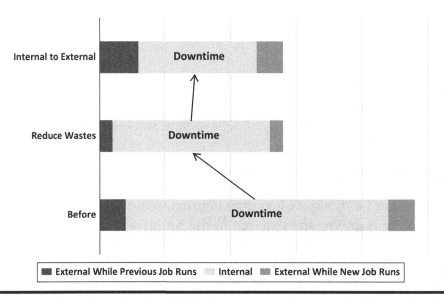

Figure 2.2   Reduce downtime by eliminating waste and converting internal activities to external activities

Stages of a Set-Up

> Preparation – the activities needing to be done or things needing to be on hand to be ready for the actual set-up.
> Set-Up Itself – the actual activities to change the process over.
> Adjustment – the activities to dial in the process to make the new product.
> Finishing the Job – starting up the process, putting everything away, and completing the necessary paperwork.

There can be wastes in any of these stages. And when there is waste, the set-up will take longer than need be.

Wastes in Preparing for the Set-Up

The biggest waste of time in most set-ups is the scavenger hunt. You remember scavenger hunts, don't you? Everyone gets a list of non-routine things that they have to collect. And the first team to collect all of them and return is the winner.

In most set-ups, pulling everything together for the set-up is like a scavenger hunt. You go racing around looking for tools, measurement devices, auxiliary equipment, paperwork, and even raw materials. And most companies conduct these searches as internal to the set-up while the equipment is down.

Waste in the Set-Up Itself

And then when they actually start the set-up, they face more wastes. At one company I worked with, they had 12 bolts holding a small fixture in place. There wasn't a single bolt touched during the changeover on that fender stamping press I saw at Toyota – the two halves were held in place with slide-in mounts and clamps. Using hand tools to screw stuff in and screw stuff out wastes time.

And the waste in walking during most set-ups probably eliminates the need for the operator to hit the gym after work on days a set-up is done.

Wastes in Adjustments

This is probably where the most time is lost in set-ups – dialing the process in. At a company that makes feed rollers for paper handling equipment, I observed a set-up person taking over 6 hours to locate the "pizza cutters" that slit the polyurethane tubes to size. There were 13 cutters to cut the tube into 12 feed rollers. All the cutters were mounted on a shaft and each was held in place with a set screw. The set-up person slid all 13 onto the shaft and positioned them 1½" apart with a tape measure. After tightening them in place, he loaded a tube onto the machine and slit it. He took feed roller 1 over to the laser mic and measured its width. The width spec was 1.500 ± 0.005 inches. He had used a tape measure to position the cutters so you know the first feed roller was not in-spec. He came back over, loosened the set screw on the second cutter a little, and tapped the cutter with a small jeweler's hammer to move it over. I asked how much he had to move it over. He responded with "about 6 taps." After the next cycle, he did two more taps and that brought the dimensions into spec. Then he followed the same technique for feed rollers 2 through 12. I'll bet some days it took him longer than 6 hours to adjust all of those cutters! Not only was he wasting time, but he was also wasting material – he used up 51 tubes in making the adjustments. And yes, I was plenty bored watching that while the video unit recorded the set-up!

At a metal cutting operation, I watched the technician spend 32 minutes tweaking the CNC program, which had been downloaded from their server. Fortunately, his cutting cycle was 35 seconds, otherwise it would have taken him much longer to dial the process in.

Waste in Finishing the Set-Up

And then just when we think we are done with the set-up, we waste more time finishing up. One firm that sputtered precious metals finished the set-up and then waited 4 hours for the vacuum chamber to pump down when changes to the pumping system could have cut the time in half. An automotive stamping company finished the set-up, made 100 pieces, and then took 5 down to the Quality department, where the sample waited in queue with all of the other quality checks being done in the plant. It would take from 15 minutes to 3 hours to get the results back and the stamping operation was down the whole time. Oh, and they only had one set-up rejected in the last year. Other common wastes in finishing the set-up are doing paperwork, which is often redundant paperwork, and cleaning up the work area/putting the set-up stuff away before starting up the process.

There are many other wastes that companies create in these four stages of the set-up. Like with any lean effort, set-up reduction requires us to eliminate the wastes. That is the first marching order in set-up reduction. The second marching order is that if you cannot totally eliminate a waste, try to minimize it and then convert the activity to external set-up time.

Rules for Set-Ups

Let's look at some rules that should be in place in all companies to minimize set-up time.

Measure the Time

Even at races with no broadcaster monitoring the pit stop down to the hundredth of a second, the chief of the pit crew uses a simple stopwatch to measure the time it takes the pit crew. Companies should do the same thing for each set-up, although it does not have to be done with a stopwatch. In addition to measuring the time, it should be recorded and plotted on a graph against previous set-ups and against the set-up target established by the company as shown in Figure 2.3.

Know What Is Coming Next

In order to prepare for a set-up, the set-up team needs to know what product or product family is coming next. Production Planning has to be proactive and let the team know far enough in advance that the team has time to prepare for the set-up before the process goes down.

Anticipate Maintenance Activities

If you are going to have maintenance activities during the set-up, figure out ahead of time what maintenance is needed or might be needed and have the maintenance crews, tools, equipment, and parts on hand and ready to go when the process goes down for the set-up.

And even if it's only "we're just going to have maintenance check it while we're down," you should be ready for the worst case. Assume it's broken

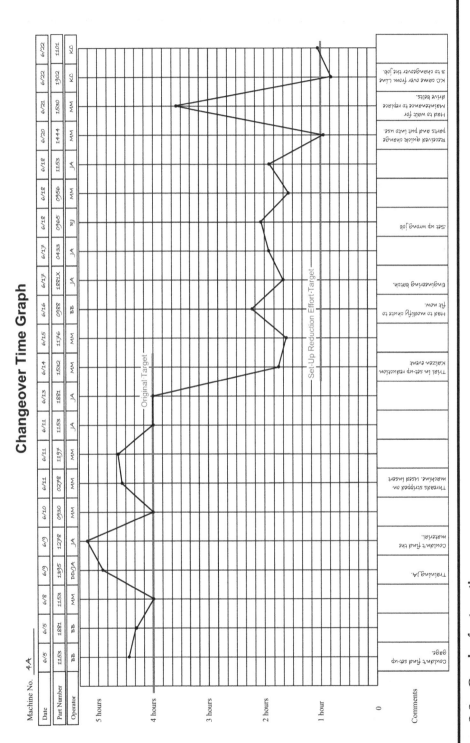

Figure 2.3 Graph of set-up times

and will need to be fixed. Have everything needed to fix the issue right at the machine when it goes down.

Lastly, figure out beforehand where maintenance is going to be working and plan the set-up around them. You might have to change order of activities and roles. Plan those out beforehand and make sure everyone understands the changes to the upcoming set-up.

Define Roles

If you use a team to attack the set-up, then each person needs their role and activities defined. One of the roles is the working leader of the set-up. Working leader means that the leader performs part of the set-up. This is not a stand-around-and-direct leader. The leader is there to provide direction when needed but is otherwise working.

The other roles should be defined in detail – what activities each person is going to do and approximately how long they should take.

Make Sure Everything You Need Is on Hand before You Start

The old 5S adage is "a place for everything and everything in its place." I will add to that the word "beforehand" – everything that you'll need for the set-up should be identified and placed in identified positions before the process goes down for the set-up. This is a good place to have a checklist of what will be needed for the set-up.

Eliminate Waste in Motion

If the workers doing the product changeover are moving around, then they probably are not doing actual set-up activities. We need to minimize or eliminate these movements. The biggest waste in motion in a set-up is often the set-up operator walking around getting materials and equipment for the set-up. In one stamping operation I worked with, before the set-up reduction activity, the operator kept his toolbox 15 feet away from the press. He walked back and forth constantly to that toolbox. Another waste in motion is constantly going back and forth around the equipment rather than making all adjustments on one side and then doing all on the other (or even better, eliminating the need to do them on the "other" side). The set-up and the placement of tools and components should be planned to minimize worker motion.

COMMON WASTES OF MOTION IN SET-UPS

- Going to the tool room or maintenance stores for parts or fasteners.
- Looking for fixtures or other set-up components.
- Walking back and forth to tool carts (look at all of the waste in Figure 2.4).
- Moving equipment to another location to make modifications to it.
- Looking for tools or gauges.
- Trying to find the supervisor.
- Looking for raw materials/stock for the next job.
- Walking around equipment.

Mistake-Proof the Set-Up

Mistake-proofing, also known as Poka Yoke, is one of the cornerstones of the Toyota Production System. Those set-ups at the Toyota facilities discussed earlier in this section were thoroughly mistake-proofed. Toyota engineers used pins or guides for locating components so that they were always in the correct position with no need to adjust them. For example, a fixture (guide) for setting tool length ensured the length was always correct.

The adjustment of the "pizza cutters" on the polyurethane tube cutting machine was mistake-proofed, which eliminated the jeweler's hammer from the set-up. The cutting shaft was machined with a fixed stop at one end. Cutting blades were slid onto the shaft separated by spacers machined down to ±0.0001 inches to produce the 1.500 ± 0.005 inches dimension every time. After adding the last cutter, a stop was tightened into position. Figure 2.5 shows conceptually the cutting approach before and after the improvements were made.

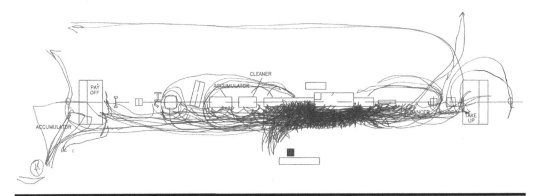

Figure 2.4   Workflow diagram of wasted steps while setting up

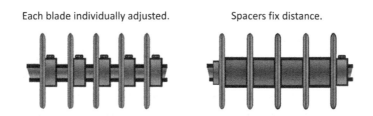

Figure 2.5   Mistake-proofing the set-up with guides

One final note on this set-up, the whole assembly of the cutting shaft was converted to external – there were two quick change shafts made and one gets set up for the next job while the other cuts tubes for the current job.

Pins and guides are great, but the best mistake-proofing methods are elimination and combination. If we can eliminate an activity from the set-up, there cannot be a mistake made in it.

Eliminate or Minimize the Need for Tools

Using a tool takes time and often, finding the tool takes even longer. If you can eliminate fasteners and other needs for tools, the set-up will go faster. Of course, tools cannot always be removed from the equation. So, if you cannot eliminate the need for tools, look for ways to minimize the number of tools you use and how often you need to use them.

Among the ways to eliminate or reduce the need for tools:

- Use clamps to secure, not bolts.
- Quick disconnects for fluid and air lines.
- If you have to use bolts:
  - Standardize to one or two sizes.
  - Use techniques so that you do not have to remove the bolts completely such as pear shapes holes or U-washers.
- Reduce the number of fasteners if it can be done safely.
- If you have to work inside an enclosure for the set-up, have hinged-access doors, not bolted-on access panels.
  - Or even better, relocate what you need to access out to the exterior of the enclosure.

Eliminate the Need for Adjustments

Adjustments, especially those done at the worker's discretion, need to be eliminated. In most set-ups, making the adjustments to get the process running properly takes more time than physically changing out the components.

Many CNC milling machines come with T-slots in their beds. Fixtures can be secured anywhere on the bed with T-nuts. This gives the operator flexibility in positioning fixtures. But here flexibility equals more downtime. With T-slots, you adjust the cutting program each time. You install the fixture, measure its location, and then calculate an offset to tell the program where the fixture is. You might have to repeat these two or three times to get the positioning exact. Going to fixture plates mistake-proofs the positioning of the fixture. This eliminates the adjustment process with the program.

You can also eliminate or reduce adjustments by removing all tape measures from your operation. If you need to make a measurement, for example, to set the length of a cut, use a stop block or mount a fixed scale with lengths pre-marked on the equipment. At a power door manufacturer, my set-up reduction team cut three steel rods to match the standard lengths that the aluminum frame pieces were cut to. We color coded them to make them easy to identify. These steel rods were used to set the length of the sawing operation. A special rack was built just under the support table to store the steel set-up rods.

And if you cannot eliminate adjustments, look to minimize the adjustments or speed them up. Consider moving to power tools to speed the adjustment process up. For example, on a sintered metal press, the ram had to be mechanically cranked up or down into place for the new part. This was a slow, arduous process because of limited access and the fine pitch of the drive screw thread. Going to a portable power tool to turn the screw saved 10 to 15 minutes a set-up, not to mention saving a lot of brute force effort on the part of the operator.

Require Standardization

Everything about the set-up should be standardized – same sizes, same components, same tools, same techniques, and same locations.

Tooling such as dies, jigs, and fixtures should have the standardized mounting locations, sizes, and general dimensions (Figure 2.6). In a stamping operation, each stamping die should have the same overall height, stock feed height, and mounting plate dimensions. If you cannot standardize all dies to the same dimensions, then create families of sizes to minimize the number of changes needed during the set-up. In a machining operation,

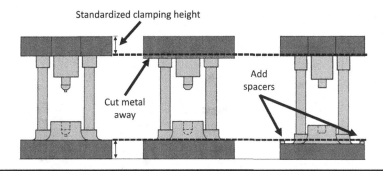

Figure 2.6   Standardize die height

fixtures should be standardized to the same base size and location. Plastics injection presses should have the molds and the cooling/heating connections standardized or a standardized frame used to pre-mount the mold.

Standardized components will lead to the same tools being needed so that the set-up crew does not need to hunt down special tools.

Part of standardization includes using 5S techniques to organize the locations of everything that will be needed for the set-up. Everyone in the organization should understand where things belong and be committed to putting things away in the proper place when done with them.

Balance Tasks

This ties in with Define Roles. If the set-up is being conducted by a team of two or more, then the tasks should be balanced. With a team set-up, the set-up will take at minimum as long as it takes the person with the longest total task time to complete those tasks. All too often set-up teams have people standing around waiting because they have finished their tasks and are waiting for someone else to be complete.

The set-up shown in Figure 2.7 originally took 260 minutes with two operators involved. The tasks assigned to Operator 1 took 260 minutes to complete and those assigned to Operator 2 took 200 minutes. Multiple times during the set-up, each operator was idle while the other one worked. If the tasks in this set-up were perfectly balanced between the two operators so there was no idle time, then the set-up would take 160 minutes, a cut of 38% without any real improvements to the set-up process at all.

But don't balance set-up task times between operators before you have improved the set-up. After the set-up above was improved, the tasks that were originally assigned to the operators would take them 20 minutes and 120 minutes, respectively. So, the set-up would still have taken 120 minutes

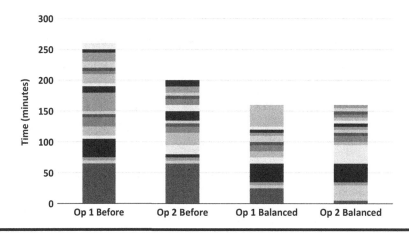

Figure 2.7   Impact of balancing set-up activities

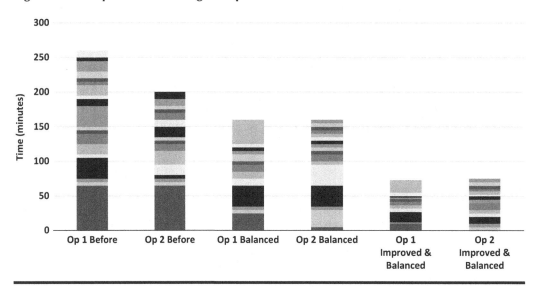

Figure 2.8   After improvement and balancing

to complete. And what a piece of cake this set-up would be for Operator 1. But by balancing the tasks between the two operators as shown in Figure 2.8, they were able to achieve a 75-minute set-up – a savings of 71% from the original 260 minutes.

To balance the tasks, identify which worker has the tasks that take the most time. Then identify how to move some of those tasks to another worker. When balancing tasks, don't be afraid to look at splitting up activities within a task.

I use a simple spreadsheet to balance tasks and I have a live graph in the main worksheet so that I can see the effects of moving tasks between workers. The spreadsheet also makes it easier to break up tasks into their activities if you need finer detail to balance the process.

Don't Always Wait for Quality Checks

Many operations require that their Quality department sign off on first-offs (a sample of the first "good" product coming out of the process). The operators change over the process, run a few parts, send those over to Quality, and wait for the results before starting up. Remember the set-up time clock is still ticking away while the process is down waiting for those quality checks. But maybe it should not be down waiting for the results. Maybe we should be running the process while the quality checks are being made.

Yes, we risk that those parts or that product might not meet the quality specifications and will have to be scrapped. But it's a risk-reward situation that you can decide using straight financial calculations. Let me offer another real-life example.

At an automotive parts stamping facility in California, over 1 hour of each changeover was the time for the Quality inspector checks on first-offs. Each stamping/finishing line just sat there while these checks were made. We started the set-up reduction activity on a line that averaged 72 parts a minute. The average manufacturing contribution for parts made on that line was 11¢ with a direct cost average of 6¢.

I went into the quality records and checked the first-off results. Their first-pass quality level for that line was almost 99% – they had five first-piece rejections in 453 set-ups in the previous year.

If they had been running while the quality checks were being made, they would have scrapped $1,296 of parts while creating almost 2 million "extra" good parts with a manufacturing contribution of $212,890 (again assuming all the "extra" parts are sold).

Now it is not always that clear cut on whether you should run or hold for the checks. But even here, the set-up reduction team had to fight the perception that there was the possibility of mixing good parts with bad parts. Even our plan to use a red barrel to segregate parts while the quality checks were being made was met with resistance. It took the executive team to overrule the production manager to enact this and save the hour per set-up.

Focus on the Bottleneck Process

In a cell, the set-up should be focused on the bottleneck operation first – even if it means diverting manpower from other parts of the set-up to this operation. Because that is the slowest operation, then it is the one that you want to be up first in a changeover. The other, faster operations can catch up later.

If the bottleneck is the first operation in the cell, this is easy. You get the bottleneck running and then you can accumulate parts downstream while completing the set-up on the rest of the line. These accumulated parts can be fed to the faster operations later when those operations are up and running. But if the bottleneck is not the first operation, you either need the operations feeding the bottleneck to come up prior to the bottleneck or you need to have some WIP on hand from previous runs to feed in to the bottleneck. You might need to do some calculations to determine if this is worth pursuing.

Now that we've seen a lot of the "what" there is to set-up reduction, let's look at a process for "how" to reduce the set-up time. And I recommend that set-up reduction efforts always begin with a team approach.

Reduce the Set-Up Time with a Team

Most organizations are looking to reduce the set-up times for existing processes. The best approach is to find the bottleneck process and attack its set-up time using a team approach. Here are nine steps you can use.

Create a Set-Up Team

Establish a cross-functional team of three to six for the set-up reduction activity. The team should include an operator or set-up person and someone from maintenance who is familiar with the equipment. You might also want team members from the tool room, engineering, and even from the equipment manufacturer. If you do have someone from the equipment manufacturer, try to get someone from Tech Service. You certainly do not want just your salesperson.

The team might also consider having invited guest members when they are working on specific parts of the set-up. For example, if they are working on ensuring that the next set-up is known well in advance, they might need the planner/scheduler to be part of those discussions.

And have at least one outside person on the team, someone who understands set-up reduction concepts, but works outside the process in question. This may be someone who had worked on the process in the past, but it would be even more beneficial to have a fresh perspective from someone with no experience on the process to ask the "why?" questions.

Once you have selected your team, train them in set-up reduction concepts or buy them a copy of this book and have them read this chapter.

Establish a Goal for the Team

Give the team a target for how much faster the set-up should be. This could be a specific time, e.g., <10 minutes (to achieve SMED) or ≤1 hour or it could be a percentage reduction. I never allow a team to shoot for less than a 75% reduction, but some organizations settle for a target of at least a 50% reduction.

Remember, the greater the target reduction, the more the team will need to focus on significant changes from the status quo. They will not be able to just tweak the existing process and achieve their goal.

Define the Process Bounds

The team needs to define what the scope of the process they will work on. Some companies will have the set-up team work on part of the process and not the entire process – for example, in a machining cell, focus only on the bottleneck piece of equipment. I do not endorse this approach. I believe that the process bounds should involve whatever process equipment and whatever support equipment (air, water, cooling, lubrication, gases, etc.) that must be changed in order to go from one product to the next.

Capture Background Information

Before starting out, the team needs to understand the process – the equipment itself and the products that run or are going to run on that equipment. This information should be collected ahead of time so that the set-up reduction team has it available at the time needed. It is often useful to put equipment information such as mold or die sizes into a spreadsheet or database program.

EXAMPLES OF INFORMATION TO COLLECT BEFOREHAND

■ Review Production Info
- Determine which products are made in the defined process.
- Which normally run?
- Which may be run?
- Current lot sizes.

■ Get Information on Raw Materials
■ Equipment Information
  – Get drawings of equipment, dies, and fixtures.
  – Compile data on equipment, dies, and fixtures.
  – Sizes.
  – Key features.

Video, Observe, and Time the Changeover

The team needs to capture the details of the changeover in order to reduce the time it takes. This should be done by videoing the entire set-up – from shutdown of one product to the start-up of the subsequent product. At the same time, all of the team members should observe the set-up and take notes on opportunities to reduce the set-up time.

Video the Set-Up

Plan the effort so that the product changeover being videoed should be worst-case. That is, in changing over between the two products, there should be as many changes to the process as possible. You do not want a simple changeover.

For example, in a molding operation, the changeover should require changes to the feed equipment, the molding compound, the mold itself, and the part removal and conveying system, not just a mold change.

VIDEO TIPS

■ The camera or cell phone needs to be secure and out of the way.
  – But you also need to see what is going on.
  – For short set-ups (i.e., <30 minutes), hold the camera.
  – For longer durations, use a tripod.
■ Remember to follow the workers – move the camera if you need to.
■ Make sure you have enough light where needed.
■ Run the camera on slow speed.
■ Have enough memory card space available or tapes on-hand to record the entire set-up.

■ Turn the date and time on.
■ No need to record during breaks and lunch.

If you only have one camera or cell phone and more than one person doing the set-up, consider videoing several set-ups and focus on each person for one video. If this is not feasible, then keep the camera focused on the most important part of the set-up and occasionally pan to the other activities going on. When there is more than one person doing the same task, for example changing mold sets in a blow molding machine, then have the camera on the operator who the team thinks does the job the best. Some people think you should view the worst, but why not learn the best techniques and then improve from there rather than starting from the bottom?

Observation of Set-Up Tasks

During the set-up, team members should be watching the set-up and noting opportunities for improving it. Care should be taken to ensure the team does not get in the way and actually impede the set-up. If the team is too large for the space around the set-up equipment, break up the team and have part of the team observe another set-up.

You will need to divide the team up if the set-up is being performed by more than one worker. The set-up reduction team should observe the activities of each person working on the set-up.

The observers should document specific tasks being performed and look for ways to reduce the set-up time. Take notes on each task, how long it took, whether it was internal or external to the set-up time, what tools and supplies were used, and other general observations. Make sure the team understands that if they think of a potential improvement, they should write it down immediately.

It might be useful during the observation to use standard Industrial Engineering techniques such as Set-Up Observation and Standard Work forms (Figures 2.9 and 2.10).

Time the Set-Up

As part of videoing and observing the set-up process, the team should take time measurements – the overall set-up time, the times for individual tasks, and any time that the equipment needs to run during the set-up.

Set-Up Observation Form

Process/Equipment						Date
#3 Filler/Seamer						10/20
Changeover From		Changeover To		Operator(s)		Observer
16 fl oz		12 fl oz		DJ		Tommy

Task No.	Description of Task	Int or Ext	Start Time	End Time	Elapsed Time	Value-Added?	Notes
1	Go to Planner's office	E	9:42	9:43	0:01	N	
2	Pick up master formulation	E	9:43	9:45	0:02	N	Start new office can put 15 oz case
79	Lower bain door	I	10:48	10:50	0:02	22%	
80	Set seamer height of seamer	I	10:50	11:10	20:00	Y	Call East Coast for ideas on reducing time
	times at the line					10%	Left for 4 min 20 sec to obtain seamer tool
132	Wait for lab evaluation of seams	I	11:54	12:23	0:24	N	
133	Start up the line	-	12:23	12:23	-	-	
134	Complete paperwork	E	12:24	12:28	0:04	N	Convert to on-line
					2:29		
					2:22		
					0:07		
					1:48		

Figure 2.9   Example set-up observation form

Total Set-Up Downtime

Again, this is defined as the length of time from the last good production to the first good production.

This measurement includes breaks, interruptions, conversations, etc. – everything from last good production to first good production. Summing the individual task times will not capture the total time.

This measurement provides the set-up team with a baseline to show progress from.

Task Times

Measure the times for each task for each person involved in the set-up. For a complex task, you may need to break the task up into its individual activities and capture times for each activity as well as the overall task time itself.

Equipment Operating Times

Measure any equipment operating time associated with each task. For example, heating and cooling times, pumping times to empty or fill a vessel, time to draw or break a vacuum, or time to move an equipment component into the proper position.

Note any overlap between the equipment operating and the operator performing an activity and how long the overlap was.

Analyze the Set-Up

Once the set-up has been videoed and observed, it should be analyzed – first to gain a total understanding of what went on during the set-up and then to reduce the set-up time.

Start by reviewing the observation notes and the data from the time observation forms to establish the major steps in the set-up. This can be done by one team member; it does not have to be done by the entire team. Capture the total time for each of those major steps.

The major steps that take the most time should be the first ones for the team to analyze because they present the largest opportunities for improvement.

Starting with the major step that took the longest, the team should view the video of the tasks and activities in that step. The goals here are to look for tasks that can be eliminated or combined with others and for wastes in the set-up and determine ways to eliminate those wastes.

STANDARD WORK COMBINATION WORKSHEET

Process: _Press 59 Changeover – Plate Removal_   Date: _25 Aug_

Analyzed By: _Jim S_

#	Task Description	Manual Task Time (m)			Auto Run Time	Time Graph
		value-add	non-value	walking	subtotal	
1	Find cart			1.1	1.1	1
2	Put tools & supplies on cart		0.5		0.5	1
3	Jog press to station 1	0.4		0.6	1.0	1
4	Talk with supervisor		2.2		2.2	1
27	Put tools away		0.5		0.5	1
	Totals	8.2	6.2	4.1	18.5	0

Legend: Manual ●——● | Auto Run ●–––● | Wait ↕ | Walking ●~~●

Figure 2.10 Standard work combination form

If the set-up is being done by a team, analyze the set-up person by person unless some of the set-up team are performing identical tasks.

Look at the times for each set-up person graphically.

Identify Tasks or Portions of Tasks That Should Be Eliminated

The first things to identify are all those set-up activities that can be eliminated. This includes both internal and external set-up activities. Anything that is not adding value to the set-up should be eliminated. One of the most common activities to eliminate is the search for items needed for the set-up. When looking at waste in the set-up, go back to the wastes in each stage of the set-up that we discussed earlier in this chapter.

Note that if you are the team leader, now is the time to challenge the status quo. Challenge the team to radically rethink the entire set-up. This is the time you may ask your "outsider" on the team to step up.

Look to Convert Internal Tasks to External

Once you have eliminated all set-up activities and wastes that you can, then look to convert tasks that are currently internal to the set-up time to external. Ask yourself what tasks currently being done with the process not running can either be done safely before the process shuts down for the set-up or after the process has restarted. Many of these tasks will be making sure everything is ready and on hand before the set-up starts, putting things away, and paperwork tasks.

Speed Up Remaining Tasks

For the tasks that remain and which must remain internal to the set-up, the reduction team should ask itself how they can speed up the time it takes to perform each task. If a lone individual is setting up, could it be done faster if additional people are added and a set-up team is created? Could new or better tools speed it up? Is there a faster technique? Can the set-up be mistake-proofed?

If you are going to use a set-up team, then be sure to balance the tasks, or even the activities within tasks, between the operators. Remember that the set-up time can only be as short as the time it takes for the operator who has longest tasks and activities to perform the work.

Look at Costs versus Payback

If your changes include new parts or equipment, then, of course, costs come into play. Your management might insist on payback calculations on the investment. This could be as simple as how many months it will take for the savings or manufacturing contribution (Figure 2.11) to pay for the improvements or other financial calculations such as Return on Investment (ROI). If you do have to make payback calculations, do not present the parts or equipment individually. Present the total cost that you need to invest for all of the needed parts and equipment against the total savings/manufacturing contribution you project as a result of your set-up reduction efforts. This will help ensure you get everything needed to reduce the set-up rather than having management perform line-item vetoes on you. The U.S. President cannot perform line-item vetoes, but a management team sure can. So, avoid getting into that situation if at all possible.

Implement the Improvements

Once the changes are determined, you must put them into place. Take the time to plan out the implementation of the set-up improvements. While this might be obvious for large equipment changes, you should also create

Costs

Tooling modifications	$54,000
Quick-change clamps	$5,000
Modify access panels	$4,500
Permanent labels and nameplates	$300
Power shears and batteries	$300
Torque wrench	$100
Total Cost	= $64,200

Annual Savings

2.3 hrs saved/set-up x 238 set-ups/year x 102 parts/hour
x $1.22 mfg. contribution/part

$$= \$68,118$$

Simple Payback

$$Simple\ Payback = \frac{Costs}{Annual\ Savings}$$

$$= \frac{\$64,200}{\$68,118/year}$$

$$= 0.94\ years \cong 11\ months$$

Figure 2.11 Simple payback calculation

a plan even for smaller changes including procedural changes. Create an action plan for each improvement that you have identified in the set-up. This could be as simple as *who* will do *what* by *when*.

If you require major changes in order to reduce the set-up related downtime, then a complex action plan will likely be needed. This will involve the use of Project Management tools such as project management software, activity paths, and Gantt and PERT charts. Creating a complex action plan is outside the scope of this work, but information is readily available on the internet.

Document, Train, and Verify the Changes Work

Once you have made the changes to the set-up and created new set-up procedures or work instructions, train the operators in the changes and then have them run through the new set-up procedures while your set-up reduction team observes. I suggest that the team video this as well and then review the video of the new set-up procedure to see if additional improvements can be made.

And the team should not just walk away at this point; the team should audit the set-up three to six months after the improvements were made. The goal here is to verify that the new set-up process is being followed and to confirm that the improved set-up times are still being met.

This audit should include a review of the set-up time graphs and any set-up notes. If any problems are observed in the audit or if the target set-up times are not being met, the organization will have to decide whether it wants the same set-up team to investigate and address new issues, the operations group to address them, or a new set-up team to address them. The choice here will depend upon the scope of the problems found.

Transfer the Knowledge

The set-up reduction team should train everyone involved in the process. It is not enough to just train a supervisor and then rely upon that person to train the workers.

Make sure you cover the off-shifts. Use team members to do the training on the off-shifts; do not rely on a supervisor or another shift to relay the knowledge.

And transfer the knowledge you gained to similar processes – at your site and at your sister sites. I worked with one auto component manufacturer where they brought in engineers from another site for an applied training workshop, and in the workshop discussions, it came out that the other site had already made a number of changes to their set-ups. They were averaging 4 hours less than the host site, but no sharing of their improvements had ever taken place. [In the workshop, the combined team beat that 4-hour difference handily. The set-ups went from almost 15 hours down to 2–3 hours.]

New Processes

All of these discussions on set-up reduction have been focused on existing processes. But why not reduce the set-up time from the beginning? Now I know that's not really set-up "reduction" per se, but you should be designing and building any new process with fast product changeovers in mind. And in some cases, you should be designing new products with features to aid in the set-up.

Start this effort right from the conceptualization phase of the process or product design. Production, Engineering, and Maintenance staff who work on existing processes should be involved with the design team on any new design, especially when looking at making product changeovers faster. This is true even if the design is being handled by an outside engineering firm or equipment manufacturer.

Summary

It takes effort to reduce the set-up times for changing from one product to another. Most of the time, once we start looking at our set-ups thoroughly, we can see the wastes; they are obvious and their solutions are too. But other times, we'll need to use that old cliché "thinking outside the box" to determine how to combine or eliminate tasks, to eliminate wastes, and to convert remaining tasks from internal set-up time to external set-up time.

Chapter 3

Breakdowns

A number of years ago, I completed a plant layout and managed the move to a new factory for a blood-collection needle manufacturer. Fascinating product – the needles blunt themselves as they enter the skin so that upon pulling the needle out, the health care provider doesn't have to worry about needle pricks. But the product's design is another story. The story here was that every time I went to the original factory, the large, automated needle assembly machine was broken down. Or at least it seemed to me that it was always broken down. It sure is hard to make needles or make a profit when your main machine is inoperable. For some organizations like this needle manufacturer, equipment breakdown causes more downtime than even product changeovers.

Now Manufacturing 101 tells us that we prevent equipment breakdowns by having a Preventive Maintenance (PM) in place. But for many companies, PM involves taking the maintenance guy with the lowest skills and sending him out with a grease gun and some oil. And how many times do companies "postpone" PM tasks because they have orders that need to get out? Neither of those is preventive in nature! But even companies with fairly extensive PM programs and which follow-through on performing the PM tasks have unplanned events (i.e., breakdowns) all too frequently.

So if companies that have fairly extensive PM programs still have frequent unplanned breakdowns, how are we going to increase uptime and eliminate those breakdowns? We are going to attack sources of breakdowns, starting when we design the process, and, in parallel to that, implement a comprehensive Total Productive Maintenance (TPM) system.

DOI: 10.4324/9781003372714-3

Designing the Process to Prevent Breakdowns

Yes, preventing breakdowns starts in the design phase for any process. The major source of breakdowns on the needle assembly machine just mentioned stemmed from the air cylinders. Maintenance replaced and rebuilt each air cylinder every 2 to 3 weeks. Their engineers had designed standard duty air cylinders into the assembly machine. A great deal of downtime could have been prevented if they had designed in heavy-duty air cylinders. These cylinders would have cost more up front, but would have avoided greater costs related to downtime. The old Fram oil filter commercial says it best – "you can pay me now or you can pay me later." And "pay me later" is usually much more expensive!

Here are some of the concepts to look at in the design phase:

- Involve the operators and the maintenance staff. They know the equipment best and can give you valuable insight.
- Use the maintenance data from existing equipment.
- If the design firm or equipment manufacturer gives you references, use them. Ask about maintenance and breakdown history for the equipment they designed or built. Be sure to ask for data, do not accept anecdotes on how great they are. Prep yourself beforehand with the questions you are going to ask.
- If you can see the equipment in use at another operation or even at the factory, take the time to do that. It is easier to review actual equipment than it is to review 2-D drawings. And seeing it run is a bonus.
- Spec long life-cycle components – work with the component manufacturers. Get facts, not opinions. You get what you pay for.
- Automate where possible, such as with an automatic lube system.
- Eliminate or minimize moving parts. Wear points on moving equipment tend to break down more frequently.
- Make it easy to access preventive maintenance points. If it is not easy to get to, people will not always perform the preventive maintenance tasks.
- Make it easy to keep clean. Try to eliminate nooks and crannies from the beginning.
- Prevent moving components from getting dirty in the first place. For example, in the case of an air cylinder or electric actuator, design the process or equipment so the thrust rod is oriented down instead of up. This way the body of the unit protects the rod itself from getting dirty.

■ Build redundancy into the process. Ask yourself if there is a way to design a parallel system so that the process keeps running while one part is being replaced. For example, if a pump routinely needs maintenance, design two pumps in parallel with isolation valving so that one pump can operate while the other is being worked on.

■ Have rigorous checks and analyses starting during the design phase of the project. Among the techniques to use are Failure Mode and Effects Analysis, Fault Tree Analysis, and Finite Element Analysis.

Failure Mode and Effects Analysis (FMEA)

An FMEA (Table 3.1) looks at each step in the process and asks what can go wrong from a safety, quality, and productivity standpoint. What can go wrong from a productivity standpoint, i.e., the failure modes, includes ways that equipment can break down.

In the FMEA, the failure modes are identified, and then the effects, or impacts, of those failure modes are rated from a 1 to 10 on a standardized scale that has been set up for the company.

Then the causes of those failures are evaluated with their frequency of occurrence rated on another 1–10 scale. When evaluating the causes and their potential occurrence, the team takes into consideration any preventive controls that are built into the process or design that can keep the cause or failure itself from occurring.

Finally, the controls that are planned or are already in place to detect the failure or its cause(s) are evaluated on a third 1–10 scale.

These three 1–10 ratings are used to determine whether a particular failure mode needs to be addressed as a high, medium, or low priority.

Fault Tree Analysis

Fault Tree Analysis can be deployed in the design stage to identify the chain of events that could lead up to a downtime occurrence. This enables the team to break the chain before the process is even started up. We will look at Fault Tree Analysis later in this chapter (Figure 3.5).

Finite Element Analysis (FEA)

This computer modeling technique identifies potential weak points in equipment structure so that the design team can beef up those areas in the design stage. Besides structural analysis, FEA can look at heat transfer, fluid flow, mass transport, and electromagnetic potential so that potential failures that can stem from those areas can be identified and addressed.

■ Make components that are likely to fail, easy to change out. There should be easy-access and they should be quick-disconnect.

Table 3.1 FMEA

Issue #	Structure Analysis: Process Step	Function Analysis: Function of the Process Step and Product Characteristic	Failure Analysis: Potential Effect(s) of Failure	Severity	Failure Analysis: Potential Failure Mode of the Process Step	Failure Analysis: Potential Cause(s)/ Mechanism(s) of Failure for the Work Element	Risk Analysis: Current Prevention Controls for Failure Cause	Occurrence	Risk Analysis: Current Detection Controls for Failure Mode or Failure Cause	Detection	Action Priority
1	Spot and Face Operation	Drill countersink to A Dimension per drawing S1991	Scrap	7	C'sink oversized	Tool misaligned	In-Process Inspection Frequency OP-00008	3	Variable Gage - Keyence IM	5	M
2			Scrap	7	C'sink oversized	Incorrect Tool	Tooling Specification Sheet	1	Variable Gage - Keyence IM	5	L
3			Rework	6	C'sink undersized	Tool misaligned	In-Process Inspection Frequency OP-00008	3	Variable Gage - Keyence IM	5	L
4			Rework	6	C'sink undersized	Incorrect Tool	Tooling Specification Sheet	1	Variable Gage - Keyence IM	5	L
5			Machine breakdown	8	Part drops into machining mechanism	Clamps not set up properly	Set-up procedure OP-00009	3	None	10	M

#	Effect	Sev	Cause	Mechanism	Controls	Occ	Detection	Det	Rating
6	Machine breakdown	8	Part drops into machining mechanism	Worn clamps	PM checksheet	8	None	10	(H)
7	Downtime for tool breakage	3	Tooling breaks down	Insufficient lubrication	PM checksheet	8	Sensor on lubricant flow	4	L
8	Premature tool wear	3	Part gets too hot	Insufficient lubrication	PM checksheet	8	Sensor on lubricant flow	4	L

- Even though it may be more costly up front, design condition-monitoring sensors into the equipment. Incorporate the Internet of Things (IoT) technology to connect those sensors to databases and the workforce so that rapid analysis and action can occur.
- If you are having the line designed and built on the outside, find a reliable firm to perform that work. Be certain to interview them carefully. Find out what brands of components they prefer for their designs and do some research on those brands if they are unknown to you.
- Have the design use brands and components that you already have in your spare parts so you don't have to carry double spares or go out and buy a unit while the machine is down. Be willing to change spare parts suppliers if the brands being designed into the equipment are more reliable than your current brands.

Preventing Breakdowns and Recurrences

So now that the process and its equipment are designed to minimize breakdowns and the process is running, it is time to keep it that way. Or even if it wasn't designed in, we still need to work to prevent breakdowns and their recurrences.

Equipment reliability generally follows the bathtub curve (Figure 3.1). The failure rate is high after the initial start-up and starts to taper down as the equipment gets broken in. Then it stabilizes for a period of time before it reaches the end of its life, the wear-out period.

Breakdowns occur even at companies with solid preventive maintenance programs in place so we need to go beyond our preventive maintenance program and look at Total Productive Maintenance.

Total Productive Maintenance (TPM)

Most people recognize TPM as Total Productive Maintenance, although there are some who call it Total Preventive Maintenance and others Total Predictive Maintenance. In actuality, TPM encompasses all of these concepts. Its goal is straightforward – to keep equipment in such condition that it runs well when you need it to run. It involves keeping the equipment clean and maintained; it incorporates greater involvement by the equipment operators; and it includes preventive maintenance.

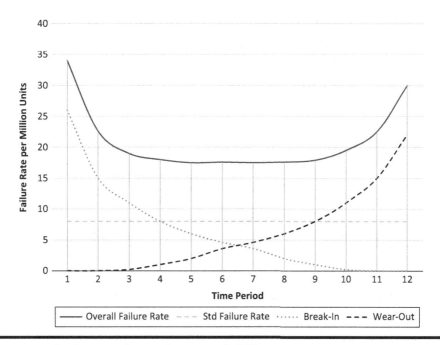

Figure 3.1   Bathtub curve for equipment reliability

Let's look at these seven elements of TPM:

■ Knowledge of your Equipment
■ Equipment Cleanliness
■ Preventive Maintenance
■ Worker Involvement
■ Preventive Engineering
■ Predictive Maintenance
■ Spare Parts

Knowledge of Your Equipment

TPM starts with developing knowledge and understanding of your equipment and how it functions. With new equipment, Maintenance and the operators should be involved from the beginning. If possible, start training them at the manufacturer's site as the equipment is being built. At minimum, have Maintenance and the operators involved when the manufacturer's tech service crew comes on-site to start up and train your company in the equipment. Make sure training related to maintenance and PM is part of the manufacturer turning over the equipment to you.

Developing knowledge and understanding includes having a good library of information on each piece of equipment and any key subcomponents. This includes the equipment manuals and your maintenance procedures as well as any information you can gather from the component manufacturers, technical journals, and internet. And if you think about your neighborhood or school library, that means the information is organized and easy to access whether it be on paper or electronic.

EQUIPMENT FILES

- Need to cover process equipment and critical components. Critical components are those that wear out or are critical to the equipment function.
- Develop an indexing system.
- Assemble start-up manuals, equipment brochures, and anything else you have on the equipment.
- If you do not have good information, try to get it from the equipment and component manufacturers.
- Talk to equipment and component manufacturers to ensure your information is up to date.
- Internet searches can lead to equipment information including manuals and videos. Include them in your equipment files even if you can find them on the internet now.
- Organize the files so that anyone can find information.
- Files can be electronic or paper, but read-only electronic files cannot walk.

I prefer electronic with read-only permissions so anyone on the team can access the information any time – and you do not have to worry about the information disappearing!

Equipment Cleanliness

One of the plants that I visited under the tutelage of Ohno san was a baby clothing manufacturer near Nagoya. Ohno san was focusing on TPM that day. Over and over that day he pounded into our heads, "Clean equipment runs better." Before they started following a model of the Toyota Production System, that plant had sewing machines that broke down constantly. Thread and cloth dust covered the machines and got into every nook and cranny.

This wreaked havoc on the moving components – it's surprising how abrasive cloth dust is. And as components wore, they increasingly failed.

Then Ohno san had the plant implement the 5Ss. He told us that they started this by cleaning several sewing machines thoroughly with vacuums and scrubbing them with toothbrushes. Then they closely monitored where the dust accumulated in these machines after use. Once they had data, they identified the sources of the dirt/dust and worked to prevent accumulations – they applied rubber seals and silicone; put some areas under a slight positive pressure with clean, dry, compressed air to keep the dust out; and set up regular cleaning schedules for the areas that they could not put preventive measures in place. The lessons learned were applied to every sewing machine in the factory. Combined with better preventive maintenance on the machines, breakdowns dropped by over 96%.

And it's not just for sewing machines. Many companies implementing and maintaining 5S programs have seen the added benefit of decreased breakdowns – especially those with rotating, sliding, and rapid-cycling mechanical components.

Many readers will have been through a 5S course or two in their careers so I'm just going to recap the steps to keeping equipment clean:

1. Train the operators and staff in 5S concepts.
   a. Sort – only keep what is needed in the work area.
   b. Set-in-Order – put what is needed in a proper place and label it.
   c. Shine – clean the equipment thoroughly and figure out how to keep it clean.
   d. Standardize – set up routine practices that everyone follows.
   e. Sustain – keep the effort ongoing and improving.
2. Start with a pilot area or machine.
3. Thoroughly clean the machine.
4. Track where it gets dirty.
   a. Use a tool such as a concentration diagram (Figure 3.2) to monitor the equipment.
   b. Be certain to check inside the equipment too.
5. Use a problem-solving approach to prevent the equipment from getting dirty.
   a. Be certain to get to the root causes before you jump to preventive measures.
6. Establish a cleaning schedule for areas that you cannot prevent from getting dirty.

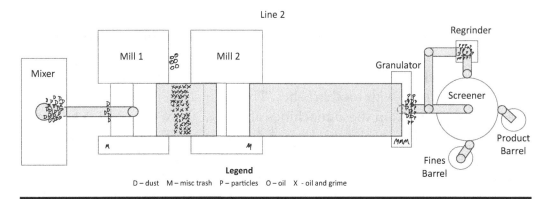

Figure 3.2   Concentration diagram

And if clean equipment starts getting dirty where it was clean before, something changed in the equipment and its components. This needs investigation using a problem-solving approach to get at the root cause and put permanent preventive action into place.

Preventive Maintenance (PM)

Cleaning is just one part, albeit a key part, of TPM activities. There are other tasks that might need to be done periodically to equipment and its components to keep the process from breaking down. There is still a need for PM. Moving parts need lubrication. Belts need to be tightened. Bearings need to be replaced. Sensors need adjustment. And there are many other tasks depending on the type of equipment that you have.

But one thing to remember with preventive maintenance – you want to minimize time down for the PM just like any other downtime. You do not want to be trading breakdown downtime for PM downtime.

One plastic molding operation had each of their 250T screw injection machines down for a shift a week for PM. They did a great job with the PM – they had almost no breakdowns – but the downtime for the PM was 20% of their capacity for this one shift operation! With a little work, we safely converted most of the PM tasks to external time, done while the machines were making parts, and cut the actual time each machine was down to just over an hour per week. They eliminated the new press from their capital plan for the next year.

Worker Involvement

Many companies have their preventive maintenance activities conducted by their Maintenance organization. The workers who operate the equipment are not involved. This is a big mistake because workers who are not involved don't have a stake in the race. Equipment problems are Maintenance's problems, not theirs. In one of the plants I worked in, shortly after I joined the site I was talking with one of the operators after a key piece of equipment broke down. The operator made an offhand comment about the breakdown.

"I'm not too surprised. It's really been screeching the last few weeks."

"Weeks!"

As far as the operator was concerned, he was a bystander, not involved at all. Maintenance should have known about the screeching and fixed it.

Within a year, he was involved. We broke down the PM activities into two categories – Routine and Skilled. Operators were trained in Routine PM tasks and were given the responsibilities to complete them. This left the Maintenance workers free to concentrate on PM activities and other maintenance tasks that needed their skills. And where in the past the operators wandered off for a break when Maintenance or an outside contractor worked on their equipment, we changed that to where the operators assisted the Maintenance crew. They were involved in their equipment all of the time. They began to take ownership of the equipment all of the time.

Implementing PM

To make this transition happen, the operators and maintenance needed to know what needs to be done, who does it, how, and when.

What and When – The PM activities themselves and the frequency that they need to be completed are determined from the original equipment manufacturer (OEM) information in your library, from talking with the OEM team, and from the experience and knowledge of your maintenance and engineering staff. Do not discount that last part – your team may have better knowledge about the equipment than the OEM does.

You can schedule the PM manually using a spreadsheet to track dates and a weekly schedule board, but I recommend going with a Work Order System (or better yet, a more comprehensive Computerized Maintenance Management System, or CMMS).

How – Methods should be developed for the PM tasks and documented in work instructions that include photos. In writing the work instructions, you may identify techniques, such as color coding (Figure 3.3) or checklists, that will make it easier to perform the PM tasks correctly.

Before finalizing the methods, try them out and observe them being used. Look for opportunities to move tasks *safely* from internal (done while

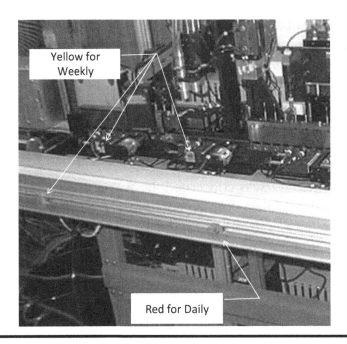

Figure 3.3   Color-coding for greasing frequency

the equipment is down for the PM) to external (done while the equipment is still running).

Who – For each of the tasks, does it require Maintenance skills or can the operator do it with or without training?

Or should the task be done by a team? If done by a team, ensure that the tasks are balanced so that no one is idle while others are still performing their tasks. This is done with the same approach as we discussed in Chapter 2 for set-up reduction.

And maybe the PM needs to be contracted out because specialized services are needed or the organization does not have the time to perform the tasks.

KEY QUESTIONS TO ASK ON PM ACTIVITIES

- Do all the operators have the skills to perform the PM activity?
- Can we reasonably expect them to learn the skills?
- Does the operator have time to perform the activity?
- Do we have the skills in-house to perform this task?
- Do we have to contract out to get the skills, hire someone, or send someone for training?

PM Education and Training

Train everyone involved in the PM – this includes area supervisors and managers who might not actually be performing any PM actions.

The training starts with classroom education on TPM concepts and then an overview of the PM activities they will perform. This education should include:

■ What is TPM?
■ Why TPM?
■ How TPM fits into our overall downtime reduction and continual improvement efforts?
■ Roles in our TPM effort
■ PM responsibilities

There needs to be an emphasis in the education and training on taking ownership and taking action.

TRAIN IN USING YOUR SENSES

Use your senses:

■ If it sounds different, something has changed. Take action.
■ If it smells like it's hot or burning, there's probably something wrong. Take action.
■ If it feels hot or like it's vibrating more than normal, it's probably not normal. Take action.
■ If something looks "funny," look into it.
■ If it tastes funny, … Okay, we're not going to use that sense other than using your mouth to communicate the issue!

This education does not qualify anyone to perform PM tasks. Once educated, operators must be trained out on the floor in the routine PM tasks that they will perform. This involves reviewing the work instruction, demonstrating techniques where necessary (and it is necessary more often than not), and observing/guiding as they perform the tasks to ensure that they got it.

And do not just assume that the Maintenance staff has the skills to perform the PM tasks that they need to perform. Maintenance should receive the same PM overview education as the operators. Then they should either be trained in their PM tasks or audited in performing those PM tasks if it is thought that they do not need training.

To verify the education and training, audit the operators and the Maintenance staff periodically to make sure they maintain (pun intended) the skills – that they continue to perform the PM correctly.

A few final words on PM before moving on:

- Emphasize safety and the safe way to perform tasks in the education and in the training. Now read that last sentence again!
- Communicate clear boundaries of freedom to the operators during the training and on the job on what PM they can do and what PM/repairs they cannot do. Be very clear!
- Make it easy and make it efficient to perform the PM. A maintenance cell adjacent to the work area with secure parts storage might be better than walking back and forth to a consolidated Maintenance area.
- Have labeled PM kits of supplies and replacement parts that can be pulled off the shelf when a particular PM comes up.
- Audit the PM activities. Add them to your audit plans and make sure the PM is being done and is being done correctly.

And back to the injection molding PM downtime example, I want to reiterate that you need to ensure you do not move the downtime caused from breakdowns to PM – work to eliminate all causes of downtime.

Preventive Engineering

Most facilities have effective safety programs to prevent accidents from occurring and they react quickly to accidents to prevent recurrences. They do not do so well in preventing breakdowns from recurring. They fix what is broken, but they fail to take the time to determine the underlying reason that caused the machine to break down in the first place and to put permanent preventive measures in place.

The same preventive engineering that needs to be done when accidents occur needs to be done for breakdowns as well, especially breakdowns that take hours to repair. The plant needs to apply a problem-solving approach to get to the root cause of the breakdown and to develop and implement a solution that will prevent the recurrence.

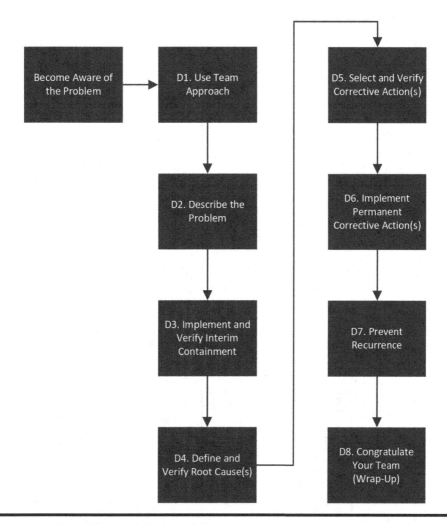

Figure 3.4   8-D problem-solving model

My go-to problem-solving approach is the 8-Discipline, or 8-D, model (Figure 3.4). It is a team-based model so it works well for larger breakdowns. And even an individual can follow the same approach, although not all of the steps will apply.

D1 Use Team Approach – assign a team of three to six individuals with the proper skills to determine the cause of the breakdown and to implement a solution.

D2 Describe the Problem – the team should describe the breakdown with what is known and not known about it. Use What It Is-Is Not analysis here (Table 3.2).

Table 3.2 What It Is–Is Not analysis aids D2 describe the problem

Is/Is Not Questions	Is	Is Not	Investigation		
			Questions to Answer	Changes	Date
What Object, Products, Technologies	Machine 82 cutting Op 30 on aero part 29066 in the T Cell.	• Other CNCs in the T Cell • CNCs in other cells used strictly for other parts		P – Mat – forging supplier Eq – Me – Env –	Feb this yr
Defect, Failure Mechanism	Downtime from chips jamming	Downtime from coolant flow restriction			
Where Seen on object, Where on lot, Where on wafer	In the chip conveyor	In the auger	• Where are chips jamming in the chip conveyor? • Exact same CNC is being used in Cincy; what is difference between them?	P – Mat – Eq – Me – Env –	
Seen geographically,	New Britain plant	Not seen in either Cincinnati or Costa Rica plants with same CNC			
When First seen	First seen after shutdown in July this year	No data showing this occurred before shutdown this year	• Did something happen to the equipment during shutdown? • What do operators do in unjamming that prevents a recurrence during lot? • How long after start-ups and set-ups does it jam?	P – Mat – Eq – replaced chip conveyor screen Me – Env –	Shutdown
When else seen	After set-up with material change (thorough cleanout) on all shifts	After unjamming, will normally not jam up again for remainder of the lot			
How Big Frequency	0-1 times per lot	Frequency could increase as the lot progresses		P – Mat – Eq – Me – Env –	
What is trend?	No data	No data			
Who Operator involved	All operators across all shifts	Doesn't occur for specific operators nor occur only on certain shifts			

D3 Implement and Verify Interim Containment – put temporary measures in place to prevent the impact of the breakdown from being felt by the internal or external customer should it recur while the team is investigating.

Interim Containment can include:

■ Temporary fixes such as the use of a metal-repair composite.
■ Running the equipment slower.
■ Stationing a "Watch" at the potential point of failure.
■ More frequent checks and short-duration maintenance activities.

Remember that any interim containment measures should be removed once the root cause is determined and the permanent and preventive mistake-proofing solution put into place.

D4 Define and Verify Root Cause(s) – tunnel down into the process and the equipment to find the underlying mechanical reason, or reasons, that the breakdown occurred.

You are playing detective here – examining all broken or worn-out parts, collecting and analyzing data, and searching for suspects.

POTENTIAL ROOT CAUSE ANALYSIS TECHNIQUES TO USE ARE:

■ Process flowcharting	■ Failure analysis
■ FMEA	■ Simulation
■ Fault tree analysis	■ Special testing
■ Five whys	■ Accelerated testing
■ Comparative analysis	■ Finite element analysis
■ Timeline of changes	■ Statistical analysis
■ Data collection and analysis	■ Regression analysis
■ Interviews	■ Design of experiments

D5 Select and Verify Corrective Actions – identify a mistake-proofing, poka yoke, solution to prevent the breakdown from recurring. Check that it is going to solve the problem and solve it permanently.

D6 Implement Permanent Corrective Actions – plan out the changes, put them into place, update work instructions, and train the operators and supervisors.

D7 Prevent Recurrence – audit the results, update documentation, and transfer the knowledge to similar processes/equipment and to any sister plants.

D8 Congratulate Your Team – report out to upper management and recognize the team's efforts.

What about that ninth box in the 8-D model – Become Aware of Problem? That's easy if a breakdown just occurred and a team or an individual is assigned to prevent a recurrence.

But you don't just have to wait for breakdowns to occur before attacking their causes. You can work preemptively. Using tools such as Failure Mode and Effects Analysis or Fault Tree Analysis (Figure 3.5), you can identify the high priority areas for breakdowns and assign a team to determine how to prevent those from occurring. This can be done with a new process as we discussed earlier in this chapter or with an existing process.

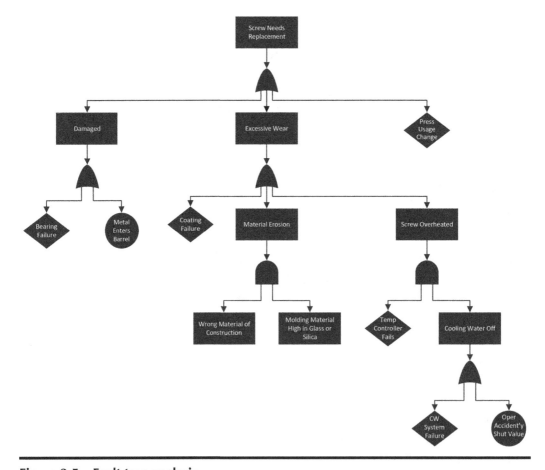

Figure 3.5 Fault tree analysis

Remember that all breakdowns are not created equal. At a polyol plant in Delaware, they spent much of their preventive engineering time on their steam system because that system had the most breakdown events. But each of those events rarely had more than an hour of downtime associated with it. If you summed up all of those hours, it paled in comparison with the 3 months that their 18" twin-screw extruder sat down when the two shafts seized and gouged the barrel or even the 2½ weeks that a crystallizer was down when it sprung a leak. So, make sure your PM and your Preventive Engineering are focused on the high risk areas for downtime.

The same will hold true for Predictive Maintenance. We will focus that effort first on high-risk areas such as our bottleneck process or key equipment.

Predictive Maintenance

Predictive Maintenance, also known in some circles as PdM, uses data and then reliability analysis on that data to determine when to act on a process or piece of equipment to prevent its breakdown. With Preventive Maintenance, we take equipment failure frequency into consideration in setting up the PM schedule. With Predictive Maintenance, we use process metrics or equipment metrics to show us when the system has changed and may be approaching failure. We work to get ahead in the game!

In some processes, quality or scrap performance indicates the health of the process. At a powder drumming operation, the level of small particles, called fines, was indicative of an upcoming screen failure. Rather than waiting for the screen to fail and having a complete system clean-out, we got everything ready for a screen change and shut down the process at the next shift change for a screen change when the fines level reached a certain value. We used statistics to determine the level of fines to set the alarm signal at. We took downtime from a 1- to 2-hour clean-out and screen change to a 15-minute screen change.

Condition-Monitoring Measurements

There are other types of measurements that can be performed on the process to predict equipment failure and associated downtime. These are commonly called condition-monitoring measurements. Among the most common families of condition-monitoring tools are:

■ Vibration analysis – rotating equipment emits vibrations and as bearings, shafts, rotors, and other moving parts wear or move out of alignment or balance, the vibration signals change. Vibration analyzers often have built-in databases to check against and then signal when action needs to be taken before a breakdown occurs.

■ Thermography – changes in heat patterns, including hot spots, can be detected on machines and their components, electrical systems, and steam piping using thermal analysis. This heating can mean that bearings are going, parts are misaligned, there is not enough lubrication or cooling, or electrical connections are loosening, among other issues.

■ Thickness measurements – taken on equipment, piping, and vessels, often ultrasonically, can indicate wear and corrosion.

■ Oil/cooling fluid analysis – changes in contaminate levels in process fluids can indicate internal wear and other problems.

■ Acoustic analysis – uses the change in equipment noise levels, especially high-frequency noise, to detect equipment problems such as bearing issues, fluid leaks, component misalignment or mis-seating, and pump cavitation.

■ Electrical system analysis – monitor electrical characteristics, such as resistance, conductance, capacitance, and frequency response among others, to identify negative trends. The techniques include motor circuit testing and analysis, which include winding and insulation testing, that look for changes indicative of upcoming motor failure.

Depending on the equipment, there are other condition-monitoring techniques and devices as well. And many devices on newer equipment can automatically dump the data into a database for analysis through IoT capabilities.

Analysis

Some condition monitoring equipment has built-in analysis. It will suggest that you act when the condition deteriorates to an action level set by the equipment manufacturer or the condition monitor manufacturer. As artificial intelligence (AI) evolves, more devices will become available and some may become capable of correcting themselves before a breakdown occurs.

Or you can hire one of the big guns in the marketplace, Oracle or IBM, to conduct your predictive maintenance effort including the analysis.

But in many cases, you will have to take on the PdM analytics yourself. As part of this, you will need to capture the history of the process performance. I recommend that you capture the time, the production point (e.g., pounds run since last data point, units made, equipment cycles run), and the product history on the process along with the condition monitor's results.

Why production point? Because some equipment failure is not tied to the chronological time lapse since the last repair/replacement, but to the quantity run on the equipment since the last repair. This is especially relevant to equipment that does not operate continuously.

The product history is important because some products are "rougher" on the equipment than others. For example, breakdowns on an extruder are going to be drastically different if you are making a phenolic brake-piston compound versus a general purpose (GP) phenolic for pot holders. The brake-piston compound with its high silica loading is much more abrasive and eats up extruder components much faster than a GP phenolic. Or take a plant using sulfuric acid – your pipe and equipment corrosion model will be much different if you are only handling 10% sulfuric acid at room temperature versus a range of concentrations up to 90% and elevated temperatures. The same is true for many processes – some products are rougher on the equipment than other products so you have to understand the product history across the equipment.

Once the data are captured, an analysis must be done to develop a statistical model, or algorithm, that predicts when the equipment or component will fail so that you can take action before that failure occurs.

To me, the analysis starts with a picture. Maybe it is simply a run chart with the time or production on the x-axis and the condition monitor's output on the y-axis. In Figure 3.6, the condition being monitored on a sieve is the ΔP, or pressure drop. When the process exceeds the specification, the graph signals the operator to shut down before a major overload that could damage the equipment occurs. Some analyzers on condition-monitoring devices have this capability built in. Tying that capability into a programmable controller can create a control system that automatically shuts down the process in a controlled manner before a breakdown occurs.

Algorithms for Predicting Breakdowns

The graphic may give some clues about the behavior of the process as it marches toward a breakdown, but our goal now is to create an algorithm

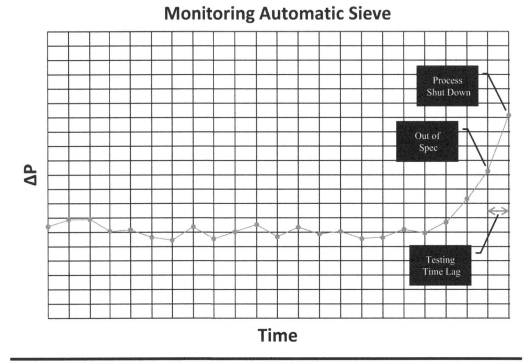

Figure 3.6   Run chart of downtime predictive measure

that will forecast when a failure could occur. We'll use the current state of the machine from our condition monitoring, our analysis on where the state of the machine is heading, and past data, including failure occurrences, for the machine or the component being monitored.

This failure occurrence data can be from your equipment history or from the OEM.

Our analysis will employ statistical techniques. Some may be quite simple. The histogram in Figure 3.7 shows the rebuild point for air cylinders on an automated assembly line. Based on these data, we will prevent ~19 out of 20 failures (−2s point for this nearly normal failure distribution) if we replace cylinders during a product changeover or other planned non-working time before 700,000 cycles.

We may have to use rougher statistical techniques such as regression analysis or time-series analysis, e.g., such as ARIMA (autoregressive integrated moving average) or EWMA (exponentially weighted moving average), to model and predict where our condition monitoring metric will be in the future and when we need to take action to prevent a breakdown. There are full books just on this topic alone so we will not go into the details on these

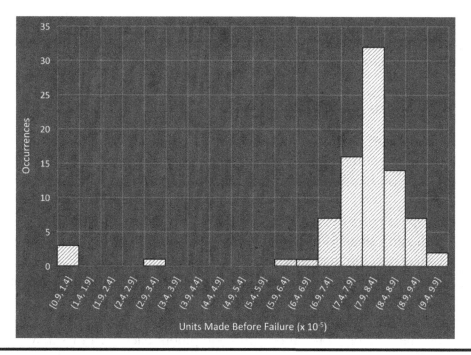

Figure 3.7 Histogram of rebuild points

techniques here. For more learning, you can take one of the many reliability engineering courses out there.

Spare Parts

Spare parts are really part of making repairs and PM, but I want to put a separate section here on it to emphasize their importance. It is tough to repair broken equipment if you do not have the parts or supplies needed to make the repairs. Yet two of the most common things to lop off at budget time are spare parts and maintenance supplies. To quote the cliché, this is penny-wise and pound-foolish.

At one of my customers, the decision not to purchase a spare for a critical component of a screw injection press has led to a press being down for almost 4 months now. So far they've lost at least $28,000 in manufacturing contribution because they didn't have a $5,000 spare. They have 8 weeks to go on the quoted lead time for the replacement part. And they have 13 other presses the same size, model, and manufacturer!

This is not to say you need to carry excessive spare parts and maintenance supplies. I personally take every OEM's spare parts list with a grain of salt. You are dealing with sales folks after all. Like your PM program itself, the spare parts list needs to be planned out. And the entire list does not need to be purchased all at once.

Plan Your Spare Parts Purchases

Start the planning process by looking at the bottleneck equipment and critical infrastructure equipment, such as compressed air systems.

Questions you need to ask in planning your spare parts include:

- What spare parts do you need on hand to perform all PM tasks?
  - You can calculate how many you need on hand from the frequency of use and the lead times.
  - Determine if you really need these on hand all of the time or can you get them just before the planned PM activity.
- What parts or subsystems might break or wear out?
  - Estimate when in the life of the equipment each part or subsystem might break or wear out.
  - Identify the downtime if they do break taking into account the availability (lead time) of the replacement unit.
  - Look at costs for obtaining a replacement on an emergency basis including emergency shipping.
  - Determine if you can substitute or modify a part or unit you already have.
- What can we afford?
  - If you can afford everything on both lists, great! And let me know because I have never run into this.
  - When you cannot afford everything on your lists, you'll need to get a budget from your management team and plan out what you are going to procure and when.
    - Prioritize your spare parts purchases using the answers and information on what is needed for PM and what might break (from the two bullets above).
    - FMEA or Fault Tree Analysis can also help prioritize.

Reduce Spare Parts Costs

"But spare parts are too expensive. And they are non-value-added – they are inventory, waste, just sitting on a shelf."

Okay, I've heard that and I can even buy it a bit. But, even so, similar to where you need some inventory as a buffer, especially before your bottle-neck operations, you need some spare parts to prevent downtime. Here are some thoughts on reducing your spare parts costs.

Standardize

At a plant I played turn-around manager for, the equipment had four different types of PLCs from around the world. The plant carried four different power supplies, four different input boards, and four different output boards in the spare parts inventory.

As part of our TPM efforts, we standardized on one PLC manufacturer and preferred model. We required our engineers to use that for any new equipment. And we set up a plan to convert the three non-standard units to the preferred one as equipment upgrades were made or breakdowns occurred.

The PLCs were not the only standardization done. We further reduced the number and types of spare parts carried by setting up lists of preferred suppliers for common components. These were then specified in our new equipment purchases. We converted existing equipment as the opportunity arose.

Sourcing

Many equipment manufacturers make a significant portion of their profits off of spare parts and replacement parts. There are mark-ups on commercial components purchased from them. A little investigation will enable you to go directly to the source or to a local distributor to purchase commercial components. You might need to purchase the initial spare part from the equipment manufacturer to capture its identity, but then you purchase subsequent spare parts from the source.

And even for parts made by the equipment manufacturer, the machine shop down the street might be able to produce an equivalent for half the price. Be sure you are aware of patent issues and understand the materials of construction before you do so.

Cannibalize

Buy used equipment at the myriad of auctions constantly taking place, bring them in, and strip them down for the parts just like the auto junk yards do with car parts.

You can do the same thing with your old equipment rather than trying to sell it or just shipping it off to the scrap dealer.

Once stripped out, be sure any parts salvaged are cleaned, checked out to ensure they function, and labeled before putting them in their designated locations in the spare parts inventory.

Make Your Own Spare Parts

One of the best plants I have seen in my work travels around the world manufactures aluminum beverage cans down in Puerto Rico. One key aspect of that plant is that they have two engineering students working part-time each evening designing/reverse engineering and making spare parts for their operations. Many of these are "wear" parts that are replaced frequently.

The spare parts work area is equipped with computer workstations and equipment – a full-size CMM, a bandsaw, a CNC machining center, a manual vertical milling machine, and a 3-D printer among others. Once made, spare parts are labeled, scanned into the maintenance system, and put away in a designated location in one of the most organized spare parts storage rooms out there. Their payback for the equipment purchases was less than a year.

Create a Purchasing Consortium

A consortium would allow you to keep only a share of the cost of spare parts on the books until the part is actually needed.

The most obvious consortium is for large companies with multiple sites to combine the spare parts purchases for those sites. Store these common spare parts at the plant with the best shipping access to the other plants. And yes, the site accountants will hate this, but it will save the company money.

For smaller companies, look to business associations to put a consortium together. If you have to do it yourself, talk to businesses in your geography that you might expect to have similar equipment.

Summary

Preventing downtime from breakdowns and subsequent repairs takes a multi-faceted approach. And it is not easy. For many companies, even something seemingly simple such as creating equipment files takes a major effort.

And that is just the starting point. Then throw in the advanced statistics for preventive engineering and the downtime prevention becomes daunting.

But if you take the task and break it up, it will not be as overwhelming. You can start immediately with designing new equipment to be more reliable and easier to repair. Applying problem-solving skills to find the root cause of breakdowns so that you can prevent recurrence is another easy step.

For PM and TPM, establish a team to focus on this effort. Your Maintenance Manager or Facility Engineer may be the obvious choice to lead this team. Get the team thoroughly trained in TPM and then have them create a step-by-step plan for the organization.

Then it becomes a matter of taking one step at a time, monitoring the plan and the results, and determining if any course corrections are needed.

Chapter 4

In-Process Downtime

It's hard for some to fathom, but you can actually have downtime while your process is "running." Sounds a bit outlandish, doesn't it? "Downtime" and "running?" When you step back and think about it, there can be some sense made from it – after all, many processes are made up of multiple pieces of equipment. You can see how the overall process could be running, but you have downtime associated with an individual piece of equipment. But I am going to go one step further and state that you can have downtime even if your process is a single piece of equipment, while that equipment is "running!"

To look at this, let's go back to our premise in machining operations – if you aren't cutting chips, you aren't making any money. Or broader, if you aren't converting the raw material into saleable product, you aren't making any money. With that said, picture how many times you have seen your process "running," but no chips being cut or no raw material being converted. That's downtime!

This can occur with processes that are being controlled by the operator or by a computer. For example, an operator could return the cutting head to a fixed point and go off to mix and add more coolant to the process. If you look at the operating log on the computer, it will look like the process was running when it really wasn't. Or the machine would be "running" according to the log while it is actually "down" because it is changing out a dull tool. It is not cutting chips while doing that.

Here's an example from a manufacturer of flexible pipes where the downtime was built into the operating program itself. The flexible pipes connect home water supplies to the faucets of large tubs. The company

DOI: 10.4324/9781003372714-4

operated one machine at a 23.3-second cycle time to convert a length of rigid pipe into a flexible one. When the demand for these pipes grew faster than anticipated, the company immediately started the process to have a second machine designed and built for $525,000. A fear arose in the organization that their customer would bring on another source or another technology if it appeared that the demand would outstrip their capacity before a second machine could be delivered.

I was working there helping them set up some manufacturing cells for other products. I heard about this project from one of their engineers and, like a good consultant, got myself work on that as well – I figured that I could get them enough capacity to tide them over until a new machine arrived and made operational.

The first thing I did was get out on the floor and observe the process closely. The machine was loaded by hand with precut pipes. These were placed onto an inclined shelf that served as a magazine. When the machine was ready to process a pipe, a pin dropped down allowing one pipe to roll down the incline into a nest. Then, chucks moved in from the sides and clamped the pipe. A small air cylinder activated to score the pipe. The air cylinder and the nest retracted. The machine processed the pipe. When finished, the nest returned and the chucks unclamped from the part and pulled away. The finished part fell into the nest. Once the chucks were in their home positions, a second small air cylinder fired and pushed the tube onto another inclined ramp that fed into a product bin. This ended the cycle. If the machine was loaded with precut pipes, it immediately began the next cycle by dropping the pin and allowing the next pipe to be loaded and processed.

After watching the process several times, it became obvious that the machine actually paused between each one of those steps. The machine was run by a PLC so I obtained a copy of the ladder diagram for the program. Sure enough, the programmer for the machine design/build firm had built in Wait steps between each activity. To me, a wait step equals process downtime in most cases. Working with an engineer familiar with programming PLCs, within an hour we had the machine operating at 16.4-second cycles – just by eliminating some of the Wait steps and minimizing others. The capacity of the machine was increased by 42%.

[That was not the end of this story though – two days later after a couple of minor machine and program modifications, we had the machine operating at 9.1-second cycles. For example, we moved the inlet pin down so it was closer to the nest – this eliminated some of the rolling time while loading the part. We reprogrammed the machine so that the chucks started to come in as the pipe rolled into the nest. The chucks even started to close before they were in their final position. With 156% capacity increase in hand, the company never purchased that second machine.]

Delays Built into the Cycle

Delays built into the cycle is my label for this pipe example. And with PLCs or CNCs or any type of digital control, short stoppages are easily built into the programming scripts by just dropping a timer in. These timers increase cycle times. They are usually put into the programs in the early stages as safeguards or to help troubleshoot. Once the program works, these timers often never get a second look to see whether they can be reduced or eliminated altogether.

If you think your automated equipment has downtime built into its program, here is a summary of the steps to use to change that:

1. Review the flowchart of the program.
   a. If you do not have one, create one.
2. Observe the process with a stopwatch in hand.
   a. Take detailed notes and record times.
   b. Video the process while you are making your observations.
   c. Look for places in the sequence where the machine seems to pause between steps.
   d. Look for sequences of operations that are being done in a series of steps rather than in parallel steps.
   e. Look for times when the machine is traveling or operating without processing the part or material.
3. Review the machine control logic/program.
   a. You might need a controls expert to work with you on this.
   b. For PLCs operating in ladder logic, you might not need to create a flowchart; just use a print out of the ladder logic program.
   c. Look for spots where Delays are programmed in.
4. Work to eliminate or reduce the Delays
   a. Always keep an eye towards safety of personnel and the machine.
   b. Start conservatively – reduce Delays before eliminating them.

5. Look for operations that can be done in parallel or at least overlapping a bit (starting a step while the previous step is still underway).
   a. Again, keep an eye on safety.

Some sources of in-process downtime might not be as obvious. These processes might need a team focused on them using a problem-solving approach to identify the sources and eliminate or reduce them. Among the areas for the team to look at are:

■ Poorly programmed tool paths.
■ Getting the process ready/time to reach steady state.
■ Machine speed is slowed down.
■ Loading/unloading the process.
■ Walking.
■ Extra operations, such as a second rinse.
■ Operator needed to start the process.
■ Scrap.
■ Excessive recycle/rework loops.
■ Assembly line or cell start-up and shutdown.
■ Conveyance issues.
■ Unbalanced operations.

Let's take a look at each of these.

Poorly Programmed Tool Paths

There is no value being added when you are "cutting air." Cutting air doesn't finish a part! Any time the cutting tool is traversing from one cutting point to another without cutting chips, there is waste in the process. As stated earlier in this section, the process may be "on," but it is not producing. Many programmers are conscientious about minimizing this waste, but it can be helpful to have a second set of eyes look at the tool path as well. And newer programs do a much better job of designing the tool path than older programs did.

Getting the Process Ready/Time to Reach Steady State

Any time the process is "getting ready" to perform its function, there is downtime. At one customer, there was 4 hours of pump-down time in a

12-hour cycle. The process was not producing one-third of the time it was recorded as "Running." Some modified ports and vacuum pump changes cut this in-process downtime to 2 hours per batch cycle.

This same type of in-process downtime occurs whenever equipment has to "get ready" – be heated up or cooled down, be evacuated or pressurized. These may be part of the cycle, but your goal still must be to minimize the time the step takes or eliminate the step.

At my plant in Connecticut, we brought in two maintenance workers (two for safety reasons – should never have one person working alone in a factory) at 3 am on Monday mornings to start up ovens that needed heat up time, compressors, HVAC, and water systems so that the plant was at the right temperature and all the equipment was ready to run when first shift punched in at 7 am.

They started up our big two-roll rubber mill at 6:30 am to give it time to reach steady state before the shift started. We had mix made on Friday waiting so that when the operator arrived, he could start running the mill immediately – no downtime.

The key thing here is to determine how long it takes your equipment/processes to reach steady state or to be ready to run and then sequence their start-ups accordingly.

Machine Speed Is Slowed Down

Another form of in-process downtime isn't really downtime at all – the machine is actually performing and adding value. But if the machine speed is slower than standard or design, then it has the same effect. You've lost production.

When this occurs, it is generally because the operator had control of the process and slowed it down purposely. This doesn't mean that the operator was sabotaging production. It may have been a necessity to get quality parts out. At an auto brake lathe manufacturer, the operators had to slow down the traverse speeds when milling castings because there were so many inclusions in the castings – this occurred after Purchasing had sourced a less expensive casting.

However, there are occasions when slowing down the machine is malicious – for example, slowing down a stamping press to make sure that the process doesn't finish before the end of the shift so that one doesn't have to start a changeover.

Whether needed changes or malicious ones, the best way I found to address this is to make changes to the machine speed visible. Automatically log the machine speed so that changes can be investigated. Or require a key from the supervisor to make the change. On one paint line, we programmed the yellow andon light to flash if the overhead conveyor speed was manually changed from the standard range for the job. That made the change obvious to everyone and the andon light being on required a planned response.

Loading/Unloading the Process

A screw machine is down during a scheduled run for the time it is being loaded with bar stock. A CNC is down from the time a finished part is unloaded until the next unfinished part is loaded and positioned. A spring machine is down while the next coil of wire is being loaded and the first springs off of it are being checked. This downtime for loading and unloading the process often goes unrecorded. The operator is working after all.

This type of process downtime should be treated just like a set-up reduction effort for a product changeover. It is the same thing, just on a shorter time scale. But the same things apply – get ready to change the material beforehand, have fixtures that minimize the number of adjustments that need to be made to properly position the incoming part, and eliminate or minimize the need for hand tools. Figure 4.1 shows a Kanban space filled with the next coils of material for the job.

In a stamping operation, adding a second unwind in front of the existing one paid for itself in less than a month in time savings (okay, so it was a used unwind. If it had been new, the payback would have been about two months).

Walking

As discussed with set-up reduction, the worker walking to find something or move something while the process is "up," but not producing, needs to be eliminated. I often see this in machining operations where the operator unloads parts and walks them over to a bin and then walks to another bin to get the next ones. While some machines capture this downtime, many times this is just considered part of the cycle and not captured or thought of as downtime. At a concrete additive facility, the process goes down every

Figure 4.1   Kanban space for pre-staging coils

pallet because the operator needs to walk around the facility looking for a fork truck to move the pallet out and another pallet in. The process was down while the operator was walking around, but the operator was considered to be "working" so that time not producing was not captured.

Extra Operations

Often extra operations come about because we needed them once for a special situation and they just stayed – like black sheep relatives visiting. We put a bandage on a problem so that we don't have to address the underlying issue. Instead of addressing why there are burrs and eliminating them, we add a deburring operation. At a high-end bicycle manufacturer, the weld finishing department for aluminum frames was larger than the welding department. A welded frame was sometimes touched by two or three finishers. Improving the welding techniques, training, and equipment reduced the number of extra operations required on a frame. Some finishing was still needed, but frames never have two or three finishing steps now.

One of my "favorite" extra operations is Sorting. There can be a place for Sorting – as an interim containment while a root cause investigation is underway or while waiting for a solution to be put into place. But it should never be a permanent part of a process. Sorting should always be considered an extra operation that needs to be eliminated.

Operator Needed to Start the Process

Recently I was working with a team at a sheeting operation for medical substrates. We had to improve productivity by 25%. In observing the process, one thing that stood out was that the infeed and cutting of the next set of substrates was not being done while the operators packaged the previous set. The lead operator did not hit the pushbutton to start the material infeed and the cutting cycle until they returned to the saw area from the packaging area. Instead of the saw cutting while they were packaging the substrates, the saw was cutting while they stood there.

The saw was well-guarded so the team decided to take the start out of the control of the operators. A sensor was added to detect when the stacks were pulled away from the saw and its output to the PLC started a new cutting cycle automatically. No more waiting for the cutting.

Automatic starts will almost always increase production over relying upon a person to do it – but note the "well-guarded" in the preceding paragraph; *you need to make sure auto starts can be done safely.*

Scrap

Throwing a part away is equivalent to having the process down with wasted operator labor and material costs for the whole time that part was being run. And sometimes the disruption to the shop floor after a valuable part or a production lot is scrapped creates downtime for investigations that costs more than even the value of that part.

The same tools we talked about in Chapter 3 for preventing breakdowns or preventing a recurrence of a breakdown, FMEA, Fault Tree Analysis, and 8-D Problem-Solving, are equally as valuable in attacking scrap. Using these tools can identify the root cause so that Mistake-Proofing can be deployed to prevent scrap or to prevent a recurrence of scrap for that cause. Here again, we want to start the use of these tools in the design phase to build a robust process from the beginning.

Excessive Recycle/Rework Loops

Any rework or recycle through a machine or process reduces its capacity. It is as if you had in-process downtime at the point the product is going through for a second, or even third or fourth, time.

Productivity for an automatic L-bar sealer was down last summer. During our team's process observation, nearly 50% of the packages of plastic-encased products had to be reworked. Nearly all the rework was due to the plastic "pillowing." With the pillows, the operators could not get five packages to fit into a carton. So, the packages were slit open and the product was sent through the L-bar sealer and oven again. The operator logs showed the process "in production" this whole time when it was "down" reworking, not producing. In this case the root cause and its solution were obvious – we moved the positions of the cooling fans installed for operator comfort so that they weren't blowing into the throat of a plastic bag before it was sealed.

A common area of downtime for rework involves labeling. I see many operations where mislabeled bottles, cans, and boxes are set aside at the end of the process. When enough accumulate, the filling section at the front end of the line gets shut down. Then the crew starts removing bad labels and recycling the denuded products back through the labeler. No net production from the filling section occurs while the rework takes place.

Rework for bad labeling often arises from the poor set-up of the labeler (i.e., not adjusted properly) or from having an ancient labeler. There may be multiple causes. This is a perfect opportunity for problem-solving teams to break down the problems, find the root causes, and attack them.

Assembly Line or Cell Start-Up and Shutdown

Many operations "run out" product through their assembly lines or cells before breaks, lunch, and the end of the shift. The lines are clear when they leave and when they return. This means you have idle equipment at the beginning of the process before the break and idle equipment at the end of the process immediately after breaks until the line is filled up. The assembly line is "running," just not the whole assembly line.

Instead of clearing the line, leave each station and any Kanban positions filled so that when the operators come back, each station can start work right away.

This may not just be a matter of stopping the line when the break bell goes off. There may need to be some changes to the process. At a cosmetics filling line, all filled jars were fully capped before the line was shut down. But all other stations were kept full. At another company, they kept boxes on hand to put over the work on each assembly table when the operators left for the day so that no dust from overhead would drop down onto the parts.

And in some operations, you never want to do this for safety reasons. In a detonator assembly line, we certainly did not want partially built detonators with live energetics sitting on the line with no one around. We cleared those lines before any breaks or lunch and at the end of the day and accepted that bit of in-process downtime.

Conveyance Issues

Don't you just hate it when you are rushing to catch a plane and your bag is hung up just inside the exit tunnel in the TSA scanner? We won't go into why the belt is stopped. But the line is open; it's operating, but nothing is being delivered. The same thing can happen in assembly lines when the Kanban quantities between operations have not been calculated correctly and sometimes in general operations.

Then there was the powder coating line conveyor that took 15 minutes and 22 positions before the first part reached the spray chamber. No value is being added as parts fly overhead to be painted. Oh, and then there were the 10 minutes and 16 positions after the parts left the cool down chamber. Sure, there was no in-process downtime as long as parts were being painted, but think of the lost production after the line was started up and before it was shut down – at the end of the production day as well as for changeovers. Our improvement team came up with a split conveyor system with a two-speed conveyor feeding from the loading stations to the spray/ drying booth conveyor. This same two-speed conveyor picks up from the drying booth and delivers the parts to unloading stations. We added loading stations and unloading stations. During start-ups and shutdowns extra operators move to staff the extra loading and unloading stations. Instead of 15 minutes of downtime before spraying, the spray booth now has the first part within 1 minute of it being loaded onto the line.

If the geography of the plant had been right, we could have eliminated the chain (and accordingly, time/positions) by moving the loading stations and unloading stations closer to the actual processing equipment. But that was not feasible there.

If conveyors are causing problems with in-process delivery, then once again this is an opportunity for a problem-solving/kaizen team to address them.

Unbalanced Operations

Manufacturing cells and assembly lines that have operations that are not balanced can also have Wait times while they are ostensibly running. This might not be too large of a problem unless the bottleneck operation is the one that is constantly in Wait mode. Remember back to earlier discussions in this book – capacity lost at bottleneck operations can never be recovered. If the equipment that is not balanced with the rest of the line or cell is not the bottleneck, then in most cases the Wait will be a nuisance, but not affect the output of the process. But it may be that addressing the unbalance can free up resources that can help the bottleneck.

Summary

Okay, so maybe this chapter seems like it was more about improving productivity than reducing downtime. I make no apologies. What is reducing downtime about if not improving productivity? A process is really down if it is in a state of not producing value. And you may have other examples in addition to the preceding ones. In any case, the elimination of in-process downtime is one of the best approaches to getting more production out of the same equipment over the same time period with the same labor content.

Chapter 5

No One to Run It

Not having an operator to run the equipment is another big source of down-time. And this is not just when the operator is out of the facility. It also occurs during the regular work day. There are many reasons that operators might not be available to run their equipment, keeping it down. They might be on break or at lunch. They may be in meetings or scheduled for another piece of equipment. Or they may even be off making an in-process quality check. In this chapter, we'll look at minimizing downtime caused by no one available to run the equipment.

Automation

This chapter could be very short – no one to run the process? Go figure out how to automate it so that you don't need anyone to run it. The end!

Think of all of the headaches that would go away!

Automation pricing continues to drop for robotics, vision systems, and other automation devices while at the same time quality and capabilities are rapidly rising. I have customers today that have automated processes using robots that their engineers created in part from 3D printed parts and a Raspberry Pi.

Others purchase used robots and re-control them with the latest electronics.

But even with those lower-cost approaches, not everyone can afford auto-mation or has an engineering staff with a robotic skillset. So I'm devoting this chapter to other techniques to keep the process running even when you don't have someone available.

DOI: 10.4324/9781003372714-5

Dealing with Breaks, Lunchtime, Shift Change, and Meetings

In the chemical process industry, equipment often runs 24 hours a day, 7 days a week. The processes are designed to be continuous. They are highly instrumented and run regardless of whether the operator is on break or at lunch or not.

For many other operations, as soon as the break siren sounds, the equipment goes down. Or even worse, it is shut down 5 to 15 minutes before the break in anticipation of break time! After all, who wants to go on break without washing up? And when the break or lunch is over, the machine doesn't start up instantaneously. It takes some time to walk from the break-room back to the workstation and to get prepared to start running again. A 15-minute break quickly turns into 30 minutes of equipment downtime and a half-hour lunch into an hour of equipment downtime.

Most operations lose another half hour of downtime at the beginning and end of a shift. Before actually starting work, the operators punch in and then move to the work area where they put away their coats, lunch, and pocketbooks/backpacks and get set up for the day. And at the end of the day, they shut down early to clean up and prepare to go home. Many times I see a line in front of the time clock at the end of the shift during what should be work time.

The most extreme case is the one I heard from a general contractor friend of mine. He was building a recreation center for a local town, but as part of the contract, he had to utilize the town staff and equipment for all backhoe work. In an excavating process, any time the backhoe isn't scooping dirt and rocks, it's process downtime. The excavating crew's shift started at 7 am. A typical day involved them arriving at the job site at 7:40 – it took a while to punch in, get the equipment ready, and drive the 2.5 miles across town in a backhoe and a dump truck. The morning break started at 9 am. At 8:30 each day, the digging crew packed up and drove off for their morning break. This included the backhoe operator driving off on his backhoe. They took their break from 9 to 9:15 at a local convenience store. At the end of their break, they drove back to the job site and set back up. They were usually digging again by 9:40. Guess when they quit for lunch – yes, 10:30 for their 11 am lunch break. Again, off they drove each day. They weren't as prompt getting back from lunch – digging usually began again at 12:15 only to stop again between 12:40 and 12:45 for their 1 pm break, and back to digging at 1:30 for a solid 45 minutes before they packed it in for the day at 2:15. They "had" to drive the equipment back to the shop, clean up, and wrap up the day. My friend kept track of this for a week and found that he was getting an average of ~3 hours of digging out of each 8-hour work day. That's a lot of process downtime for breaks and lunch! He's not bidding on work for this town anymore.

Employee involvement activities also keep equipment from running. Sometimes it is more fun to be off working on a problem-solving team than it is assembling units or feeding the equipment beast. Even shift meetings, safety meetings, and status meetings cause equipment downtime.

I won't even go into the amount of time lost for bathroom breaks and unofficial smoking breaks! Well, maybe I will later.

The answer to dealing with these types of downtime is easy – chain the operators to the equipment. It worked for the ancient Greeks on their trireme vessels, didn't it? Obviously a little deflecting here – throwing out a ridiculous solution to dealing with the very toughest component of process downtime.

Yes, this is by far the very toughest component of process downtime. It is a cultural issue in the organization. To reduce this downtime is about changing the culture and changing long-term employee habits. This is never easy and will be met with resistance from most workers, including your management team.

Before talking about the cultural issues, let's first look at some techniques for eliminating or reducing downtime due to breaks and shift change.

Just Keep It Running

If you have equipment like a stamping press or an automatically fed machining center, there is often no real reason that it needs to be shut down for breaks or shift change. Many operations already have enough sensors on their equipment to allow one operator to run multiple pieces of equipment.

If this is the case, why not just run the process unattended for break time? And there is no reason other than culture to shut down for shift change to begin with so keep it running then too.

To keep it running, there may need to be some modifications to the equipment. For example, feed hoppers may need to be enlarged to have adequate stock for the break time. Or the company may want to install sensors and vision equipment to enable supervisors and engineers to monitor the process or have it shut down if there is a problem during the time the operator is away.

Stagger Breaks and Lunches

To keep the bottleneck running, use cross-trained operators to keep running during breaks. Have coverage during the regular break and lunch times and have the covering operators take their breaks and lunch either before or after the regular break and lunch times.

Relief Operators/Water Spiders to Cover

Some large operations have found it advantageous to have a position of relief operator. These operators cover for meetings, breaks, and lunch. They can also be used to cover for vacations and sick leave – avoiding the costs of overtime pay.

And this might not even need to be a separate position. Lead operators are often used to fulfill this role. They oversee the line and they also fill in where needed, when needed.

The downside of this is of course the cost of benefits packages for relief operators. But the payback for doing this is often still there when the product made can be sold – the manufacturing contribution from the product made and the saving from overtime avoidance more than pay for the cost of benefits for the relief operators.

Team Coverage of Bottleneck Equipment/Operations

Whether you have manufacturing cells or still have departments, you can still use team coverage to ensure that a bottleneck never goes down. This will require some cross-training to be done for team members so that there are many operators who can run key equipment.

Cross-training starts with defining what tasks need to be performed in each job. Then the skills needed to successfully perform each task need to be understood so that training can be designed and completed. A cross-training matrix (Figure 5.1) is a useful format for capturing who has the skills to fill a specific job and who needs additional skills to learn a new job.

Once the team is cross-trained, allow them to decide how the bottleneck is to be covered so that it does not go down for breaks, lunch, or shift change. Only get involved if the team has a dispute. You should set some ground rules for the team that job tasks need to be rotated so that everyone gains experience on the tasks and keeps their skills active.

Shift Change at the Machine

When I worked in a chemical plant early in my career, the shift change was done at the machine while the machine was running. The operator did not leave the process until the oncoming operator was there and up to speed. This evolved to where the oncoming operator would show up 15 to 20 minutes before the end of the shift and spend 5 to 10 minutes with the outgoing operator. After getting up to speed on the equipment and schedule status, the oncoming operator would take over and the outgoing operator would head to the locker room to change and go home. They didn't even punch time clocks. The operators were professionals and treated each other as such. If they were going to be late or absent, they called the supervisor and almost always called the operator they were to relieve to give them a heads up.

Pay Overtime for Meetings/Meetings at End or Beginning of Shifts

Have all meetings at the beginning or end of the shift and use overtime to enable the machines to be kept running. You might not need to have overtime coverage for all employees involved in the meeting – you could just focus on the key bottleneck processes.

Shorten the Work Week

Bet you are scratching your head again on this one! But if you are a one-shift operation, you can improve your uptime by going from five 8-hour days to four 10-hour days. You have one less set of start-up/breaks/lunch/

Employee Training Matrix Rev. 3

Job Tasks / Employee	Maura	Jim	John	Bob	Steve	KC	Kevin	Flor	Lee	Cindy
BASIC SKILLS										
Data Entry	(in training)	(in training)	Q							
ISO 9001 Training				T						
Plant Safety Rules	▨	▨	▨	▨	▨	▨				
Print Reading	Q	Q		Q	Q	Q	Q	Q	Q	Q
Insp, Meas & Test Equip Use	Q	Q		Q	Q	Q	Q	Q	Q	Q
Internal Auditing				▨						
CNC Programming		Q								
Forktruck Operation	T	Q		Q	Q	Q	Q	Q	Q	Q
Material Handling	T	Q			Q	Q	Q	Q	Q	Q
RECEIVING PROCESS										
Receiving	Q	Q	Q	Q	Q	T	Q	Q	Q	Q
MACHINING PROCESS										
Manual Machining	Q	Q			Q	Q	Q	Q	Q	Q
CNC Machining		Q					Q		Q	▨
Deburring		Q				Q	Q	Q	Q	Q
WELDING PROCESS										
SS Welding	Q				T	Q				
CS Welding	Q				T	Q				
Certified Welding	✕	✕	✕	✕	Q	Q	✕	✕	✕	✕
Helium Leak Testing	Q				Q					
POLISHING/GRAINING										
Polishing	Q	T						Q		Q
Graining	Q	T						Q		Q
PACKAGING PROCESS										
Wrapping and Skidding	Q	Q			Q	T	Q	Q	Q	T
SHIPPING PROCESS										
Shipping Paperwork	Q	Q	T							
Shipping	Q	Q			Q	T	Q	Q	Q	Q
OTHER (Write in)										

Qualified as OPERATOR — Q

In Training — ◿   1-Jul

Qualified as TRAINER — T

Not Qualified - operator may not perform this task — ✕

Task is required, not yet taken — ▨

Task effectiveness verified by annual review — ▨

Task effectiveness verified by supervisor authorization — ▥

Task effectiveness verified by testing — ▤

Task effectiveness verified by 3rd party certification — ▦

EXAMPLES

Operator is trained and qualified as a Trainer, and holds a 3rd party certification. — T

Operator is trained and qualified as an Operator, and a supervisor has a record of having judged the operator's training as effective. — Q

Operator is undergoing training; when complete, will require verification during annual review. — ◿

Figure 5.1 Employee cross-training matrix

shutdown to deal with. Let's say that your team starts up the process in 15 minutes and shuts it down 15 minutes early for clean-up. They have 30 minutes for lunch and two 10-minute breaks a day with 5 minutes lost on each side of those getting to/from the break area. On a 5-day basis, you have 2 hours of downtime per day or 10 hours per week – 25% of your capacity. Going to 4 days per week cuts this to 8 hours per week – a gain of 5% of your capacity.

Satellite Break Areas

I've made several references in this section about the process being shut down early for breaks and lunch and workers coming back late from them. This occurs in many manufacturing facilities. But the length of extra time taken seems to be a function of the size of the facility; more specifically, how far the lunchroom is from the work areas. One way to minimize this is to have satellite break areas – a place just off the work area where the workers take their breaks (and lunch if desired). This saves the time walking to and from the lunchroom way across the building.

　If creating a satellite break area, there are some considerations to be taken:

- ■ Isolate the area somewhat – with partitions or even racks and cabinets.
- ■ Put a table with seats in the area.
- ■ Have a water fountain or, even better, a hot/cold water dispenser (either bottled or piped).
- ■ Install a coffee machine or coffee pot there.
- ■ Be sure to plan out how the area is going to be 5Sed.

Dealing with Downtime Due to Meetings/Projects

Another frequent source of downtime is when the operators shut down the process for meetings or projects. Sometimes this is done without the planner, or even the supervisor, knowing it is coming.

Define Allowable Time for Projects and Team Meetings

I mentioned earlier that some consider it more fun to be off working on a team or on a project than being at their machine running it. If they happen to be running bottleneck equipment, that is time you will never make up. For operators on critical equipment, I always set up boundaries of freedom for teams – we want the production operators to participate, but they are really the only ones in the plant adding value and paying all of our salaries. So all project teams had participation boundaries defined up front to them along with other boundaries such as spending, reporting, communication, and safety/regulatory. In my plants, I've had it that no operator could spend more than 2 hours per week on team projects or at team meetings without pre-approval by the plant Steering Committee.

Decide Whether to Release an Operator or Not

Just because an operator is on a team should not always mean that the operator is released from their job for a team activity. There may be some circumstances where the operator can't afford to be released. But these circumstances should be defined as part of the boundaries of freedom given to the team at its start-up. Management needs to define up-front situations where an operator might not be available to a team.

As part of this, the supervisor must have a process for keeping an operator from team meetings and activities. At minimum, the supervisor needs to communicate to the operator and the team leader as far ahead as possible why the operator needs to remain on the job.

Part of the boundaries of freedom given to any team needs to be that the team needs to let all supervisors know in advance when an operator will be away from their process for a team meeting or to work on a team assignment. And the team, operator, and the supervisor all need to know in advance under what circumstances can the operator be kept from attending team activities.

Have Meetings at the Machine

Look at whether stand-up meetings can be held at the equipment so that the operator(s) can attend the meeting while the equipment is still running. Not all meetings are conducive to being held out there while the equipment is running, but some, such as problem-solving meetings or safety meetings, are naturals to be held right there at the machine, especially if there are long cycle times.

Pay Overtime for Meetings or Project Time

Have the operators work their full shifts and pay them overtime to attend mandatory meetings, such as safety meetings or communication meetings, before or after their shift. Or an alternative to this would be to pay another shift overtime to come in early or stay late to run the equipment while a meeting was held.

The company could take the same approach with projects. If an operator has to be away from their operation to perform a project task, then plan the timing so that either the operator can perform the task on overtime or overtime coverage can be arranged.

Dealing with Quality Checks

In-process quality checks by the operators are great. They give real-time feedback on whether the process is running well or not. They help make the operators responsible for the quality of the products they make. And they help tell the operators when to adjust the process and when to leave it alone. This is much better than the Quality Department being responsible for the quality checks, and therefore "Quality," when that department cannot actually affect the quality.

But in-process quality checks by the operators can take time away from feeding the equipment and keeping it running. At one polymer components facility, I walked out on the floor and there was a queue at the laser mic. Three operators were standing there behind a fourth who was measuring her parts. All four of their processes were down because their equipment had finished the cycles. There were four machines all waiting to be unloaded and reloaded. And all four were considered by the operators and their managers to be "running" because after all, the operators were "working."

After capturing the downtime for these quality checks, we were able to justify another standalone laser mic and for one higher-volume process, a customized laser mic to measure the component on the machine as part of the process cycle.

The best in-process quality checks are those that are simplified so that they can be done within the cycle of the machine. This way the checks won't be the source of any downtime. To do this, the test equipment needs to be located at the machine or very close to it. The test needs to be done quickly – with fixtures and automatic data capture if necessary. The test should also be mistake-proofed so that it cannot be done incorrectly.

If you deal with automated processes or long cycle times, there is enough time for the operator to make their checks and this concern on downtime during quality checks will be minimal. But for manual operations, such as assembly, and for short-cycle operations, this downtime can be significant. Here are some approaches to eliminate or reduce that downtime.

Move Test Equipment to the Work Area

Eliminate the time taken to walk to test equipment by positioning the test equipment at the workstation or by positioning a satellite quality area out on the production floor. If the workstation or the quality area is laid out properly, the test equipment or quality area will not be in the way.

In some operations, test equipment, especially equipment such as a Coordinate Measuring Machine (CMM), is in a separate Quality Department area. The operators must walk back and forth to the Quality area taking even more time away from actual production. Look for alternative measurement techniques and systems that can be located out on the floor.

Buy More Test Equipment

Companies do not like to spend money on test equipment. After all, aren't quality checks non-value-added? But if having more test equipment for mandated/needed quality checks can decrease equipment downtime, the purchase becomes justified.

Buying two laser mics at the polymer plant was not inexpensive, but the payback for the two was 7 months. We also spread out the laser mics strategically in the department to minimize operator walking distances to them.

Automate Testing

Taking the operator out of the measurement itself will also minimize downtime. This can be done with software, with hardware, or a combination of both.

Some automation in quality testing has been around for decades, but the rapid development in CMOS and other sensors and in processor speed has led to automation in numerous measurement devices that could not be affordably automated in the past.

If you still cannot afford to purchase the test equipment automation, look at doing it internally. One of my customers had an engineer automate one of their measurements with a "homemade" rig that looked as professional as anything out there. It took a couple of servo motors, a slide mechanism, some parts he made on his 3D printer, and a microcomputer. For less than $225 in parts and the engineer's time, they eliminated 4 of the 5 minutes of downtime for each hourly check.

If you cannot fully automate testing, at least automate the data capture and the control chart or run chart of the data.

Permanent Test Fixtures

The hunt for test fixtures or the need to assemble test fixtures can also lead to production downtime due to quality checks. Having fixtures ready-to-go saves the operator time away from the machine.

The waste in not having test fixtures available arose at an aircraft engine part repair facility as part of a 5S effort. When the team defined the tools and support equipment needed at each workstation, they identified that additional test equipment and fixtures were part of the needs. They reported that too much time was spent with equipment down while the operator searched for the text fixture for the SOP-mandated in-process check.

The team solution was to set up each workstation with the same tools and with test equipment/fixturing assigned to that workstation. All was organized with labeled locations at the workstation.

About six months after working with them, I received a nice letter from the company president thanking me for the work. He just wanted to let me know of the benefits they achieved as a result of the 5S event including that productivity rose by 7%. Upon investigation, he wrote they found the root cause was that the operators were not leaving equipment down while they searched across the plant for a test fixture.

Another customer purchased a larger CMM than was needed for the size parts they were running. They used the larger bed space to semi-permanently position high-use test fixtures. They were always ready for use. There was no set-up time when the operators came in to measure their parts on the CMM. The only wait would be if the CMM was finishing another part when the operator came in.

Eliminate Quality Checks

Determining the frequency of testing needed with a new product is often just an eWAG (if you don't know that acronym, it is e for engineering and G for guess). Companies routinely perform quality checks every half hour or every hour with no real basis for that time frame. Once decided, the operators perform quality checks for all products at the same frequency. And most organizations never look at that frequency again, for new products or old. But the time between making quality checks should be based on the product and the performance of the process for making that product. If testing at a half-hour interval for a product always shows results in-spec and the process in-control 99.73% of the checks, then why not reduce testing to every hour and eliminate half of the quality checks? After some history at 1 hour, can we move to every 2 hours and get the number of quality checks down to one-fourth of what they were originally?

Another trick to eliminate quality checks is to look for correlations between quality checks. For a transmission torque converter, we were able to eliminate almost one-third of the dimensions measured every hour by showing statistically significant correlations with other dimensions.

An offshoot of eliminating quality checks is to eliminate the operator performing the quality checks, i.e., go back to the approach of Quality for quality checks and Production to get the product out. I have never been a fan. Use Quality to audit results, but I want the onus on making good product to rest on the shoulders of the operator(s) making that product. This is not always possible, but I am looking at all of the other approaches discussed above for eliminating downtime due to quality checks before I am reverting back to Quality performing all of the checks.

Covering for Absences/People Scheduling Issues

Sometimes there are just not enough trained bodies to run all the equipment that is scheduled – either key people are out for vacation, sickness, or personal reasons or more equipment needs to be run than on a typical day so you wouldn't have enough people even with everyone in.

Overtime

The obvious answer is to use overtime to cover absences or the need to schedule and run extra processes. Yes, one of the most hated words in any business, "overtime." No one can afford too much overtime, but as a short-term solution, some level of overtime to minimize process downtime may be needed (and for companies who have done a great job balancing operations and minimizing labor waste, some level of overtime will actually yield optimal labor costs).

Remember that overtime needs to be planned out and overtime usage needs regular review by management. Too many companies are haphazard about overtime. It needs to be justifiable – someone is out and orders require the overtime to make the production that they would have made or we need to get this order out and we need to run extra equipment to do so.

Often people eat up overtime. But there are occasions where everyone refuses to work the needed overtime. At most companies I've worked at, a reasonable level of overtime is mandatory. A company cannot abuse this or you'll create disgruntled employees very quickly. But requiring a certain level of overtime availability from employees is a legitimate business approach. If you haven't done it before, how you assign it and how you are going to introduce it to employees needs to be well-planned. Offer to work with employees who have childcare or elder care issues. If you establish a requirement for overtime, be sure to communicate this up front when a new employee is hired. And always try to give as much advance notice as possible.

Cross-training

For covering absences and handling people scheduling issues, having multiple operators who can cover each operation also reduces downtime just like it does for keeping the bottleneck always operating.

That jet engine component manufacturer mentioned back in Chapter 1 is not the only manufacturing facility to have problems with not enough operators trained to perform critical jobs.

That solution was easy – cross-train two other operators in the cell to be capable of operating the broach to make a good part and then to have them periodically run the broach to maintain those learned skills.

Besides keeping bottleneck equipment running and covering for operators who are absent, I'm a big fan of cross-training because it ensures that key skills and tribal knowledge are "backed up" in the organization. But it takes a process to have an effective cross-training approach and it takes someone being responsible to manage this process.

A cross-training process needs:

- A responsible person assigned to manage it.
  - This is typically the head of human resources.
- A list of all the jobs.
- For each of those jobs, a breakdown of the skills needed to perform the job effectively.
- A list of all operators and a breakdown of each of their skill sets and what jobs they can perform.
  - Need to define the evidence that will be required to assure an operator has a skill set or perform a job – by currently performing the job by function, by supervisor sign-off, by having passed a test or certification, or by demonstration.
- Review each job to identify any job where we do not have enough coverage.
- Identify potential candidates for performing jobs where we currently do not have enough coverage.
  - Note that union and/or employee morale considerations may come into play here.
- Defined training approach to provide a skill.
  - Including how the successful achievement of a skill will be evaluated.
- How frequently each employee needs to perform a job to maintain the skill set?
- A way to maintain the "inventory" – i.e., the cross-training matrix shown in Figure 5.1.
- How often do we need to repeat these steps?

Temps

Temporary employees can also provide coverage for absences and unstaffed operations. However, most of the time, temps aren't just "plug and play." The use of temps needs to be planned out. First, determine which jobs that you'd be comfortable with temps doing. Yes, most of the time, temps fill jobs requiring the lowest skill levels.

SCHEDULE

Positions: Set-Up | Quality Tech | Filler | Capper | Carton Prep | Inserter | Cartoner | Labeler | Mat'l Handler

Scheduled: Jacq (Out) | Mark Louie | ClaienMae | Dani | Ret (Temp) | Pascale | Chris | Jill | AJ

TRAINING MATRIX

	Jacq	Mark Louie	ClaienMae	Dani	Ret	Pascale	Chris	Jill	AJ
cGMP									
Department Safety Rules									
Level 1 Training									
Level 2 Training									
Quality Checks									
Labeler									
Setting Up									

Figure 5.2 Cross-train across skill levels to allow temps to replace someone who is out

But not everyone in these lowest skill level positions will be temporary workers. There are normally some that are permanent workers. Cross-train a few of the lowest skill permanent workers so that they can work "up" if someone is out at a job at the next skill level. You can cascade this approach up the skill levels.

Let's look at how to handle when our Set-Up Operator will be out. You can't just bring a temp in for that slot – the Set-Up Operator needs too many skills. But by having already cross-trained employees, we can move up someone with the set-up skills and backfill their spot (Figure 5.2). We keep repeating that until we get down to a low skill level position in the organization that we can fill with a temp. This enables you to add temps for whomever is out. You bring in a temp at the lowest level and then move people up your chain as needed.

Absenteeism for Sickness/Health

Sickness also causes workers not to be available to run their processes and equipment when you need them. And if you have paid sick days, that is incentive enough for some to call out sick. You need people well and at work.

On the other hand, you never want sick, contagious people sucking it up to drag themselves to work. They aren't going to be that productive. They might not be that attentive (i.e., risk getting hurt). And they are probably going to get others sick as well so you could have more people out.

Wellness Programs

The key here is to work on the preventive; emphasizing wellness. Some argue that wellness programs help improve health and accordingly reduce absenteeism. Others indicate that they have little impact. One paper that was published in *Health Affairs* by a group of Harvard researchers reported that wellness programs reduce absenteeism by nearly 2 days per employee per year with a labor savings that was 2.73× the cost of the programs. The paper implied that they didn't think this was a great return, but to me, if I can pick up 2 days of production per year per employee, I'm implementing a wellness program. Think of the manufacturing contribution being added to those labor savings.

> At one of the plants where I ran an engineering group, we set out to improve attendance. Part of our effort was an annual health fair featuring health screenings and flu shots for all employees. We had a University of Connecticut associate professor in for talks with employees on health and nutrition (his first one was *How to Live to Be 150*). He set up an individualized exercise and nutrition program for anyone that wanted one. We implemented a smoking cessation program that as a by-product also reduced unofficial smoking breaks. Our wellness efforts along with attendance policies and monthly communication at our plant-wide meetings improved attendance across all levels in the organization.

Paid Sick Days/Time Off for Being Sick

Many companies don't want to think about paid sick days or paying people when they are out sick. Some cities and states require it. Altruism aside, I'm convinced it is better to have sick people stay home. How many times have you seen a stomach virus running through your shop or office? If Patient Zero would be willing to stay home for a day or two, then very likely you would save lost labor hours overall. Not to mention that it could prevent you personally from getting sick as well!

If you do elect to give people a specific number of sick days, I recommend that you pay them for the days they don't use or you allow them to carry those day over to the next year (up to a max). That should save you from overtime pay for someone covering for them when they aren't sick, but are using up their sick days.

Paid Vacation

Same principle here as with Paid Sick Days. Allow workers to carry over or be paid each year for unused vacation time. This will save costs for overtime coverage.

One note here is that I am not in favor of allowing all of one's vacation time to be worked. While it may seem beneficial to the company to allow this, workers need time away from the job to recharge or productivity and safety performance suffer.

Attendance Metrics/Attendance Policy

Instead of covering for absences, a better approach is to minimize absences. This begins with measuring attendance, which should be one of the KPIs for every HR department. Performance levels and trends should be reviewed by top management and communicated to the workforce regularly. If the data show that an attendance problem exists or that the data are trending in a negative direction, then management needs to address the issue immediately before it worsens.

The approach you take depends on what the data show – are there general attendance problems or are there "special causes of variation," i.e., are certain people out an extraordinary amount?

Few companies do not have an attendance policy that addresses frequent absenteeism. But many companies do not enforce the attendance policy, or selectively enforce it if they have one.

If you do not have an attendance policy, establish one and communicate it to everyone, both during site-wide meetings and in writing. If you have an attendance policy, then you communicate that it going to be enforced. Either way, you should have everyone in the organization sign that they acknowledge the attendance policy and have new hires sign it on Day 1.

This is not meant to be Draconian but to enforce the attendance policy. Enforce it fairly and even-handedly. All too often managers and supervisors turn a blind eye to attendance issues with their "good" employees. Playing favorites can wreck morale. But not enforcing it at all can wreck morale even faster.

A CARROT INSTEAD OF A STICK

Some schools have perfect attendance awards. The few without an absence receive a special certificate at the year-end awards ceremony. A portion of the schools even give a small reward to the students with their certificate.

This recognition/award approach is certainly worth considering as part of your attendance policy. Some companies have used it successfully to help turn around a culture of high absenteeism. I have never implemented this myself because I have never been able to overcome two big downsides in my opinion. The first downside I think of is that you may have employees who are sick or injured showing up for work and ending up with others sick or the employee themselves worse off – especially the closer they are to achieving the reward. And the second is how do you ever end this approach without affecting morale?

Poor Safety

I have mentioned that you need to ensure tasks are performed safely several times so far in this book. Starting out in the chemical process industry, I was taught that safety is Job 1, not "Quality is Job 1," not productivity, not customer satisfaction. The 650-employee plant I worked in had three OSHA recordables in the 2 years I worked there. Only one of those occurred out in the plant.

Altruistically, we want no one to get hurt. But poor safety efforts impact operations as well as people – quality, productivity, and morale all suffer along with the person. And downtime goes up.

The accident that occurred out in the plant resulted in two operations going down – one for the operator himself and one for the operator who volunteered to drive the injured employee to the hospital to get stitched up. When Big John slipped on the ice in the parking lot earlier in the year, it shut down a whole department as the entire crew had to help the emergency responders lift him onto the gurney and into the ambulance. And it took Big John two weeks to return to work from his concussion. Two weeks during which we had several occasions his process went down for a portion of his shift because we couldn't get coverage.

A good safety program will reduce accidents and near misses and save downtime from injuries and lost time accidents. But it goes farther than that – my theory is that the same discipline that goes into creating and maintaining a good safety system permeates the facility and helps drive quality and productivity, including downtime minimalization. The key elements of a good safety program include:

- Management commitment and active leadership.
- Establishment and communication of safety policies and rules.
  - Building these rules into all work instructions.
- Safety monitored as a KPI and performance communicated regularly to the workforce.
- An active safety committee with work floor involvement.
- Regular safety training.
- A hazard assessment process such as FMEA and HAZOP for new and existing processes that drives preventive activities.
- Full accident investigations.
  - With an emphasis on true preventive actions to prevent recurrences.

With hundreds of books and articles focused strictly on safety, I won't go into details on these elements. The key thing here is to recognize that you need a good safety program for all workers as part of your downtime reduction efforts.

Culture Change

Many of the ideas on staffing in this chapter (and many ideas in the other chapters too) will require a change in the culture of the organization. The operators fought the change in the plant when we "took away" the hour at the end of the shift that they used for shutdown and clean up. Even something as straightforward as staggered lunches have upset people in some organizations. What do you mean that I can't eat lunch and socialize with my friends every day?

Although this isn't a book on cultural change, I want to leave you one idea on implementing culture-related changes like the ones mentioned in this chapter. I learned this from the vice president whose plant I took over after he was promoted. His approach, paraphrased, was:

■ Tell the shop labor committee what's coming 2–3 months before the change will be made. Tell them what and tell them why in all honesty. Ask for their input (not for their approval).
■ Repeat this to the labor committee 1–2 months beforehand. Tell them any changes you made as a result of their input or tell them why you didn't use their input.
■ Tell all employees about the change at the monthly plant communication meetings 1–2 months before implementation.
■ Repeat this at the monthly meeting just before implementation.
■ Have someone follow-up with employees immediately after implementation to learn if there are any problems with the approach.
■ Make any adjustments necessary and then communicate to employees what changes were made based on their feedback at the next monthly meeting after the change.
■ Don't mention it again. It is now part of the way we "do it."

Changes in the plant made by our team went much smoother following this approach and it has worked well for me since then.

Summary

You can reduce changeover times, prevent equipment from breaking down, and reduce in-process downtime, but if the operators aren't at the machine to run it, then all those improvements don't get you much production. Focus on keeping the process staffed during all the times that you need the process to be available. In some plants, the times when the operators are away from the machine add up to be the largest single source of process downtime. This too needs to be systematically addressed just like any other source of downtime.

Chapter 6

Supply Chain Problems: "For Want of a Nail…"

Just as with no operators being available to run the process, if the right materials in the right quantities are not available when needed, then the process goes down. We may not lose the kingdom, but we will have downtime as the operators change the line over to another product that has materials available or they wait until the material arrives at the line.

Reasons that the supply chain causes downtime abound. They exist in the plant as well as in the material supply chain upstream. Material issues include:

Internal Supply Chain Issues
- They cannot be found in the plant so the process goes down while the hunt starts.
- They fail to get delivered to the line in a timely manner.
- They were never ordered or not enough were ordered.

External Supply Chain Issues
- The supplier does not deliver when promised.
- The quality is poor; it cannot be used.
- The customer orders erratically or out of the blue so the plant's not ready.

DOI: 10.4324/9781003372714-6

     – Materials are on allocation or otherwise not available.
     – The shipper does not deliver on time.

Even the end of the supply chain, the plant waste streams, can cause process downtime.

And it is not just direct raw materials that can keep equipment or processes down. The materials involved may be consumables, such as processing aids, or even packaging supplies. At one manufacturer of medical instruments that I worked with, their line kept going down because they would run out of a key adhesive that they used on the assembly floor. And at a cosmetics contract manufacturer, one filling line was held down while the plant waited for a promotional sticker that the printer had promised to overnight for 8 am delivery – it got there at just after 3 pm, costing them nearly a shift of production.

Let's look at some of the issues with the supply chain that cause downtime and some ideas on how to deal with them. We will start with the internal issues because they should be the easier ones to tackle.

Getting Product to the Line

You have the materials in the plant, you know you have the materials in the plant, and yet those materials do not reach the line when needed. This happens even to plants with fancy ERP systems that monitor warehouse positions and activities. But like with any other computer application, it's GIGO – Garbage In, Garbage Out. One Friday night I hired a private plane and paid a grievance because our major automotive customer insisted that they were out of parts and that their assembly line would go down the next day without them. I ran out to the closed warehouse, filled my van with boxes of parts, and drove to a small local airport. Our customer received the parts by 2 am Saturday and the assembly line never missed a beat. Of course, Monday morning they "found" over 40,000 of our parts that hadn't shown up on their inventory report.

ERP certainly has its place and its benefits, but I prefer combining it with Visual Management techniques whenever possible. This is especially true for small to medium-sized manufacturers who lack the sophisticated systems of a major manufacturer or fulfillment center. But as my example above shows, even the big guys with multimillion-dollar ERP systems face downtime caused by supply chain issues.

Cannot Be Found in the Plant

The hunt is on. The inventory shows we have X quantity of ABC on hand, but on hand where? I have two operators and a supervisor searching. The ABC is not in the location shown in the material management system.

This is where a visual management system can enhance an ERP system to eliminate the search. ERP manages the high levels of control while visual controls/kanban manage the lower levels.

Designated Locations/Signs

I do not believe in the randomized storage that many ERP/MRP systems force upon you. I want my people to know which area stores which raw material so they can go to that area instantly – no search involved. Posted maps of the warehouse locations help reinforce this knowledge. I want them to follow the 5S workplace organization mantra of "A place for everything and everything in its place."

That seems simple enough, but there needs to be an effort to do this and do it right. To put this in place for your materials:

■ Decide what raw materials need to be stored and where – most fre-quently used raw materials should be closest to the use point.
■ Organize where you are going to store raw materials.
■ Mark off the locations and label them with signs to keep it visual.
   – Use posted maps for reinforcement.
■ Utilize kanbans to refill the spaces as they are emptied.
■ Create the organizational discipline to maintain the system.

Trailer Storage at Docks

I am not a fan of tens of trailers strewn around the property and folks con-stantly running outside to get materials or store them. However, if you lack space in the plant, then having trailers parked at docks and pulling materi-als out of them is a viable tactic. If they are still on the trailer, the operators certainly know where they will be.

At a paper converting company, we designed the warehouse and dock area to have three kanban "spaces" for trailer loads of three types of paper rolls. The operators always knew to find the rolls in these three trailers. There was no searching through a storage area of paper rolls.

And the system was set up so that when the roll with the red stripe was pulled off a truck and moved into production, the supervisor notified the paper supplier and another trailer load was put on the road. The red stripe was placed on a roll at a precalculated position in the trailer that allowed the replacement trailer to be filled and to arrive before the plant was out of that paper type.

Not Delivered to the Line in a Timely Manner

Sometimes materials are not delivered to the line when needed even when it is known where they are. I've seen this during changeovers where the operator leaves in the middle of the set-up activities to go find a fork truck and then move the materials for the next job to the line. Other times there has been no material handler around to get the materials. That person is busy somewhere else or was laid off in the last round of cost-cutting measures. The line goes down in the middle of a run and sits idle while waiting for the operator to page or call the material handler and then for the material handler to find the material and move it to the line.

Every company needs a golden rule – all materials need to be at the line before the line needs them. And they need the discipline to follow that rule. This needs to be the responsibility of the line. But the systems need to be established that make it easy for the operator to accomplish this every time, and the planner/scheduler needs to be proactive in that system.

Andon lights can help the line personnel manage their materials. These lights should be highly visible to the entire line. They signal the operator or material handler to bring more material to the line. They also notify the team leader or supervisor to keep an eye on the situation. The best solution uses sensors to identify low levels of material and activates the andon light early enough that material can be brought to the line before the line shuts down. They can also be set up where the operator flips a switch to light the lamp and signal a material handler. With both solutions, they can also be set up to not only light the andon but also to send text messages to the cell phones of the operator, material handler, and/or others.

Keep It Stored Near the Use Point

Raw materials and WIP should be stored at the use point wherever possible. They do not need to go into a warehouse or a locked stores position. In fact, when I am setting up a green-field plant, I work to eliminate the need for a centralized warehouse for raw materials and WIP. And you do not even need a centralized warehouse or locked stores for valuable materials. These can be stored at the use point in a locked container or cage if necessary.

If you do not have the space to store all of the raw materials and WIP needed at a process line, then you will want to store some materials at the line – typically a shift's worth or a day's worth. And you will need to set up a system to replenish those materials.

A Lean supermarket location near the use point is one viable technique. As with a food supermarket, the materials in the plant supermarket are replenished from the main warehouse after the operators have pulled materials out for use. The replenishment can be done by kanban or kanban spaces. Some plants have a material handler or water spider (see Inset) who is responsible for refilling the kanbans. This can be a full-time position or part of someone's duties.

MATERIAL HANDLER VERSUS WATER SPIDER

Both the Material Handler and the Water Spider positions have the same purpose – to keep the process supplied with everything it needs and to remove from the process all the materials that are not needed.

A Material Handler is often a low-level, entry job. The person is assumed to have no skills other than the ability to read and drive. Physically the person must have enough strength to pick up goods and haul goods around. That's the job – just like NPR's *Car Talk* chauffeur, Picov Andropov, they move when called or when they get a signal from the process.

A Water Spider is a higher level job and can be a critical part of a Lean initiative. In addition to being able to read, drive, and have the physical strength to move goods, the Water Spider also needs an integral knowledge of the process or processes they are responsible for. Yes, "responsible." Their job is to keep the work flowing. So, if a machinist needs a particular tool from the stock location, the Water Spider needs to understand machining enough to know the tool. If an operator is having difficulty fitting a component into an assembly, the Water Spider needs to understand the assembly process well enough to determine if the operator is doing something wrong or if there is a problem with the components. I personally call this position a Team Leader and not a Water Spider, but we do love our Lean buzzwords, don't we?

The material handler makes regular runs around the plant or through their process and fills the kanbans. This is called a milk run – the kanban is like an empty bottle of milk. When I was a child, the milk man came

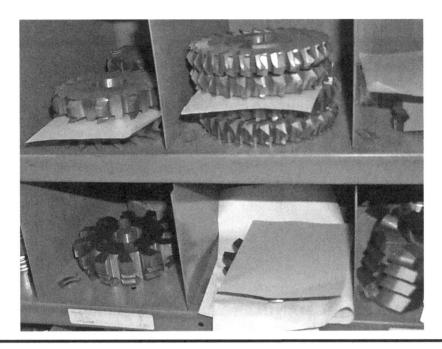

Figure 6.1   Kanbans in tooling signals when to purchase more

Monday, Wednesday, and Saturday to handle five growing boys. When my mother left three empty bottles out (three kanbans), the milk man replaced the empties with three full bottles.

The kanbans to be filled by the material handler in the plant milk run can be cards (pull the cards and leave the material to replace them), empty containers (replace the empty with another container with X units inside), or empty spaces (replace with a pallet of Y units). Figure 6.1 shows kanbans setup for tooling. When the kanban is reached, the material handler refills the bin with that cutting tool.

Kanban spaces on the floor are for larger items, such as steel or aluminum coils for stamping operations. Again, these should be right at the point of use. That space should never be left empty for long. Whenever empty, a new coil needs to be brought in from the warehouse so that the material is in place before it is needed.

Poor Planning

Planning translates from the customer order or forecast to the shop floor with the supply chain in the middle. What we call "poor planning" is most often a symptom of something else – for example, inaccurate sales forecasts, inconsistent customer orders, poor suppliers (or poor cash flow to pay suppliers), and artificial inventory pressures.

But there are instances where downtime is caused by the planning process itself. Even something as simple as the Planner not communicating the next job to the manufacturing team can lead to downtime as they wait to learn of the next job or as they scramble to change over to a job they just found out about.

We looked at some of these areas in preceding chapters and sections of this chapter. Let's look at some potential solutions to issues that we have not covered and how they could potentially improve downtime.

Does Not Get on the Weekly Schedule If the Materials Are Not There X Days in Advance

Remember, this book is all about reducing equipment downtime. Not allowing a job to get on the final schedule until all materials are in will reduce downtime. But I do not view this as a long-term strategy. It is more of an interim containment tactic as you work to improve your suppliers.

If the company is constantly losing production time because materials are not on site and schedules have to change at the last minute, which often creates some downtime, then it might be worthwhile establishing a policy that a planned run moves out in the schedule if the materials aren't on hand X days before the run. This might not service your customer as well as holding the line down until the truck shows up, but it will reduce downtime. And remember this is just an interim containment strategy.

The value of X depends on your tolerance and the ability of the planner to reschedule the line without downtime. For some companies, X is the Friday before. For others it is a week in advance. In the cases I set it up while we worked on the supply base, I used 2 days in advance.

Better Communication from Planning

A frequent cause of downtime that I see stems from poor communication by Planning to the shop floor. The shop floor does not know what is coming next so they do not have the equipment and materials for the next job out on the floor ahead of time. It is critical that the Planner be part of the plant floor. At one truck brake manufacturer, they have their Planners (and their supervisors and engineers) clustered out on the shop floor in the area of the cells that they support. It is easy for the Planner to get to the lines and it is easy for the line operators to get to their Planner.

Having desks out on the shop floor may not be feasible for many companies, but the Planner must spend time on the floor and be in constant communication with the floor. It may be archaic in this age of electronics, but I am a fan of whiteboards that everyone involved in the line can use to communicate. And one section on that whiteboard should be isolated for Planning to communicate what product is coming next.

Another area of communication that is weak in some companies is between Planning and suppliers. Part of this is that larger companies frequently have Buyers in between the Planners and the suppliers. Direct communication is always better than indirect. Use your Buyers to negotiate prices and terms and place orders, but let the Planners communicate directly and release materials against the orders.

Develop Solid Forecasts

Good sales forecasts are critical to good materials planning. Now this will not be true if you can call up today and get whatever materials you need tomorrow, but most companies aren't that fortunate. For those less fortunate (i.e., most of us), the better the sales forecast, the better the planner is going to be able to forecast material demand and ensure the right materials are on hand when needed.

But forecasts are constantly the source of jokes in many companies. Isn't "accurate forecast" always used as an example of an oxymoron? The truth is that most organizations do not work at forecasting or at getting better at it. The forecast or the numbers making up the forecast are simply plucked out of the air with no one accountable for their accuracy.

Sales Forecasting

Everyone in operations knows that salespeople are notoriously optimistic – every job is a big job and all jobs are almost sure bets. Many salespeople complete their forecasts of customer demand by gut feel with little in the way of science. With sales forecasts driving raw material forecasts, this makes creating accurate raw material forecasts and having the right materials on hand tough.

Work needs to be put in to turn the forecasting approach into a science. This starts with customer communication – constantly keeping a finger on the pulse of their business and the marketplace. You may not want to forecast for all customers and products, only the top ones. Use the Pareto

Principle and its 80–20 rule to focus efforts on the top customers or the top products that make up most of your business.

The forecasting system needs to not only involve creating the sales projections but also analyzing the forecasts and constantly working to improve the approach. This requires statistical analysis of forecasting accuracy and forecasting performance for each salesperson and each customer and giving the salesperson feedback on their performance. As you gain history, you can use the statistics from the analyses to adjust the forecasts.

At minimum quarterly, forecast monthly sales for at least a year out. I prefer having the sales team update forecasts each month. They should break down forecasts into existing customers/products and new customers/products.

- Start with orders on the books and evaluate those for potential changes in timing (both for being pulled in and pushed out) or quantity.
- Add to that the forecasts for existing customers/products – quantities, timing, and probability.
- And the third portion of the forecasts should cover new customers and new products. Again, estimate the probabilities of gaining this additional business.
- Use the probabilities of getting the job versus actual sales as a tool to improve future forecasts.

As part of the analyses, evaluate the accuracy of the sales projections from your customers as well. You can help them improve their accuracy by providing feedback.

Pay for a Sharp Planner

In some manufacturing companies, the planner is someone who was in operations and is no longer needed in that role. The planning position announcement describes that they were given the position because "of their knowledge of the shop floor." But often, it is just a place to park them. They are put into the position with inadequate supply chain training and are expected to keep the shop floor humming along smoothly. Sometimes it is a success. But often it is an abject failure.

Professional planners/inventory control folks, who are highly trained and highly motivated, can pay for themselves very quickly. Get someone who is APICS-certified by the Association for Supply Chain Management or if you cannot, get your planners into certification training programs quickly.

That's the highly trained part. And getting someone highly trained is critical. But that is not the end-all, be-all. I threw "highly motivated" in there as well. That is why you cannot have someone just parked in the job. The Planner must be self-motivated to get out there on the floor and work with the operators, to work with suppliers, and to work with management. Too many Planners let the job come to them rather than being proactive and using their knowledge to help the floor function more effectively and efficiently.

Supplier Problems

Everyone in manufacturing knows that if your suppliers perform poorly, you are in trouble. It is hard to overcome poor-quality inputs for your processes. And it is even harder to overcome those inputs not showing up when you need them in the first place. The expectations of your supply base should be 100% quality and 100% on-time delivery with good communications to boot. Unfortunately, it seems that many suppliers fail to live up to expectations without the customer's direct involvement.

This involvement needs to start with preventive measures – finding good suppliers, close by if possible, and establishing partnerships with them. And if a problem occurs, you will need to work with your supplier to fix the issue – or you need to fix it without them.

Preventing Supplier Problems

Preventing problems with suppliers starts with having good suppliers, preferably good suppliers with sites nearby. The customer-supplier relationship needs to be viewed as a partnership from both sides. Clear communication, including regular discussions of performance, keeps the partnership healthy and maintains personal relationships that are the foundations for the inter-company relationship.

Selecting Good Suppliers

Identify the Characteristics You Need in a Good Supplier

Selecting good suppliers starts with defining the characteristics a good supplier for your company must have (Musts) and those you want the supplier to have (Wants).

Potential Characteristics for Musts and Wants for a Supplier

Total cost	Operational redundancy
Terms	On-time delivery performance
Capacity availability	Minimum order quantities
Business size compatibility	Continuous improvement/lean
ERP system	efforts
EDI systems	Development capabilities
Reputation	Customer service
Values/ethical compliance	Shipping options
Location(s)	Their suppliers/supply chain
Flexibility	Environmental issues
Lead time	Regulatory compliance
Quality/productivity metrics	Value-engineering ability
Quality system registrations	Complaint rates
Safety performance	Warranty claims

If you have a long list of Musts and Wants, look for opportunities to pare the list down, but do not pare it down just because of its length.

Identify Potential Suppliers

Once you have defined the Musts and Wants, create a list of potential suppliers to evaluate against those characteristics.

Your existing suppliers (the good ones) should serve as your starting point. Approach them either to expand on the materials they supply to you or to obtain their recommendations for a supplier. If you need to continue the search, then move on to internet searches, attending trade shows, contacting trade associations, and networking.

If you are the 800-lb gorilla in the room, i.e., you are a large company, look for smaller firms as potential suppliers. Your firm will have more importance to them that should earn you more attention from them. But remember your goal – you want them as a good, reliable supplier that delivers good quality product on time to you. You want them as your partner. Your goal is not to beat them up on price because of the leverage you have with your size and importance to them. Over my career, I have experienced a modus operandi for many large companies of them using their size to squeeze small suppliers to the point of harm; they hold a warped view of "partnership," which is truly needed with key suppliers to prevent supply issues and the resultant downtime.

Smaller companies may want to look for potential suppliers that are hungry to grow or want to break into the marketplace rather than the #1 or #2 player in the marketplace.

And whether you are large or small, I recommend you do not consider competitors (or potential competitors) as a potential supplier. Too much information gets shared in a good supplier partnership and you know that their top priority will always be themselves.

Evaluate Potential Suppliers

A Decision-Making Matrix approach using your Musts and weighted Wants (Figure 6.2) can help the team identify a top candidate or candidates from your potential supplier list. I use a spreadsheet for this decision-making evaluation.

The evaluation involves conversations with the companies on your Musts and Wants and in many cases site visits or audits and data review (do not accept anecdotal evidence). It is critical that the potential supplier come away from these conversations with a clear view of your needs and that you come away with a clear view of their capabilities.

Pricing is always a key consideration so once the potential supplier has a clear view of your needs, have them price out the material(s). This may be negotiated later once you have narrowed down your list of potential suppliers. That's when it is time to negotiate and work out details.

The potential suppliers should provide prototypes or product samples for your team to evaluate in actual use. Never just rely on data sheets to determine the suitability of a raw material. The evaluation should include a direct comparison between the new materials and a control material from your current supplier. I find design of experiments (DOE) as a good technique to use for sample and prototype evaluations.

Remember that if a potential supplier does not meet one of the Must characteristics, that should be an automatic disqualifier. But with a catch – if a supplier misses on one or two Musts, but evaluates highly against the Wants, I approach them to discuss their willingness to implement the Musts they are missing. If they agree and we end up selecting them, I get that in writing and make it part of any supply agreement.

After reviewing the potential suppliers against the Musts and Wants in the Decision-Making Matrix and testing samples, obtain references from those remaining in contention and talk with each reference. Like any interview,

Musts	Acme 1	Meets Yes	Meets No	Acme 2	Meets Yes	Meets No
Located within 250 miles of plant.	186 miles	X		47 miles	X	
In business at least 5 years	12 ½ years	X		6 years	X	
Solid safety program	OSHA IR = 3.2	X			X	
No legacy environmental issues		X			X	

Wants	Wt.	Acme 1	Score	Points	Acme 2	Score	Points
Low price – target $ ■	5	$ ■	6	30	$ ■	10	50
Low MOQ – goal 1,000 units	5	10,000 units	4	20	12,500 units	3	15
Low lead times	5	4 weeks	6	30	4-6 weeks	5	25
Back-up capacity	1	Sister division in CA	8			9	
Veteran owned	1	Yes	10	10	No	0	0
			Total	573		Total	422

Figure 6.2 Example of a decision-making matrix

plan out the questions you want each reference to answer, use good listening skills, and ask follow-up questions. Use what was learned in discussions with the first reference to modify your questions as needed before talking with the other references.

Select Supplier and Negotiate a Supplier Agreement

The choice of suppliers may be obvious at this point, but it may be that the team needs to whittle the list down to one or two. Time to bring out the Decision-Making Matrix again.

Complete the final negotiations with the remaining potential supplier(s) and come to an agreement on price, terms, quality, and delivery requirements. Agree upon any safety stock requirements – either for finished products for them to hold for you or for long lead time raw materials that they need to hold to be ready for your orders. Once an agreement has been made, this all needs to be documented in a formal supplier agreement so that no misunderstanding on requirements arises.

Manage the Relationship

Once you select the supplier and have a supplier agreement in place, set up lines of communication including EDI systems for orders and inventory control. Roles and communication responsibilities on both ends should be well-defined.

From there, the partnership with your supplier needs to be managed. I will talk about supplier partnerships in a couple of sections, but remember how critical regular communications between companies become.

Shrink Supply Chain Distances

Distance creates its own set of supply chain problems. It makes delivery harder, especially up north in the winter. It makes communication harder. And it makes partnerships and cooperation harder – it is easier to cooperate and help face-to-face than it is over the phone, by e-mail, or even by video conferencing. Location is one of my key factors for selecting a supplier.

Toyota is famous for having its plants in Toyota-shi surrounded by its suppliers. Honda in Maryville, Ohio, has the same approach. Shorter distances cut transportation costs and headaches, but just as importantly, improve communication and make it easier to prevent problems or prevent them from snowballing.

When a national-brand beverage operation planned a bottling facility near Phoenix, they negotiated a long-term contract with a bottle supplier.

To minimize the supply chain distance, the two companies agreed to locate on adjacent sites in an industrial park. Now the two facilities share an automated rail car that shuttles between the two buildings. They also share real-time data on bottle usage so that the planners in the bottle plant know when to expect the rail car back to be filled again and the upcoming bottles they need to plan for. If there are any issues, the planners and engineers just walk next store and work on them together.

I always try to avoid stretching the supply chain across the big ponds with incoming materials. I like the Toyota approach of local suppliers. However, when I bring up local suppliers, the first thing I normally hear is "But the price I'm paying from Timbuktu is so much less than I'm paying now for a US supplier." That lower price does not make goods or add value while the materials sit on a container ship over the horizon off Long Beach or in one that sank in an Atlantic hurricane (both true events for two different customers of mine).

Yes, the price may be lower, but again, what is the true cost of ownership? That's what counts. Just looking at the price does not take into account all of the costs associated with extended transportation, having to deal with long lead times, and lack of flexibility, not to mention the costs of dealing with quality problems should they occur. In addition, as globalization expands at an increasingly rapid pace, the price advantage overseas will gradually shrink.

With local suppliers, you can set up kanban systems and/or milk runs. A kanban system with your supplier is no different than one in your plant. When a predetermined quantity of materials or supplies is used up, a kanban signal is sent to the supplier to signal more materials, the kanban quantity, need to be shipped in or come in on milk runs. This is known as a variable-time, fixed-quantity milk run.

There can also be fixed-time, variable-quantity milk runs. An example of this is with fasteners. Many fastener companies will set up supermarket bins in your processes and replenish them on a weekly basis. They replace whatever fasteners you used in the preceding week. In another example, the truck shown in Figure 6.3 arrives at the plant on Monday, Wednesday, and Friday each week and picks up one to three pallets of parts. This factory is the first stop on its milk run.

One thing to note – the term "local" is subjective and what is "local" depends upon your size. If you are buying in truckload quantities, then you can afford longer variable-time, fixed-quantity milk runs. However, wherever possible, keep it within a short drive.

Figure 6.3   Local milk run truck picking up parts. *Photo courtesy of Otalite Co., Ltd.*

Supplier Partnerships

A study by Kuo et al. on the relationship between lean practices and manufacturing performance found that "customer involvement" and "developing supplier" [sic] had the greatest impacts on manufacturing performance of the lean tools (P <0.001) (Kuo, Shen, & Chen, 2008). This indicates that supplier partnerships are critical to lean successes including in downtime performance.

But "supplier partnership" is one of the most misused terms out there. True partnerships rarely exist. Frequently, "partnership" is the term executives of large manufacturers use in reference to their smaller suppliers as they jam cost-cutting measures down their throats.

Partnership does not mean that you don't negotiate and don't look after your own position. But true partnering requires working to create a win-win situation between your supplier and your company. And part of that win-win becomes materials when you need them for your operation.

The key to partnerships is regular communication meetings. These should be multi-level – executives meeting executives, planners and buyers meeting customer service and sales, quality and manufacturing meeting quality and manufacturing, and R&D with R&D. By spreading these meetings throughout the year, the partnering companies constantly communicate.

Supplier Report Cards

Quarterly report cards for suppliers can be a valuable communication tool to grab their attention whether you have a partnership with the supplier or if you are just buying commodities from them. These report cards should measure performance in:

- Quality
- Delivery
- Cost
- General (areas such as customer service, communication, development activities, and flexibility)

An example of a supplier report card is shown in Figure 6.4. Each area is rated on a 0–5 scale with higher being better performance. The overall rating is obtained from a weighted average of the four categories with Quality, Delivery, and Cost each receiving a 20% weight and the General category receiving a 40% weight.

The Quality rating is derived from performance in batch acceptance and in quality issues. For this company, a 98% or higher batch acceptance with 1 or less quality issues and 0 supplier corrective action requests (SCARs) earns a 5. Batch acceptance of 95%+ with less than three quality issues and one SCAR receives a 4. No supplier to this company has ever received a 0 for quality, which would be given for less than 50% batch acceptance or more than three SCARs.

Delivery performance is also a direct measurement. For this report card, the customer controls shipping, not the supplier, so the "Delivery" rating is based on the actual shipping date versus the promised shipping date ± 1 day.

Cost and General performance are subjective ratings. Cost is a consensus score from specific Purchasing and Finance personnel. They determine a score from 0 to 5.0 for their "best" supplier from a cost of ownership standpoint and then rate the other key suppliers relative to that rating. The General performance ratings are averages taken from the ratings of all personnel who have interacted in the quarter with the supplier for the subcategory. For example, only R&D personnel rate the development activities subcategory. The averages of the personal ratings create the ratings for each subcategory and then the subcategories are given equal weight to create the overall General rating.

Supplier Performance Appraisal

Supplier   Acme   **Period**   2Q

Quality Performance – 20%

No. of Batches Shipped	No. of Batches Approved	% Acceptance
22	22	100%
Number of Quality Issues	No. of SCARs Issued	No. of SCAR Actions Received
1	1	1

Delivery Performance – 20%

No. of Line Items Shipped	No. of LI Shipped On-Time	% On-Time
16	16	100%
	No. of LI Shipped Complete	% Shipped Complete
	16	100%

Cost Performance Rating – 20%   4.0   out of 5 maximum

General Performance – 40%

Customer Service	3.9
Development Activities	--
Communication	3.9
Flexibility	4.0
Inventory Control	4.0

Overall Rating | **4.2** |

Notes   No planned development activities this quarter.

Figure 6.4   Supplier report card can grab the attention of the supplier's top management

Supplier report cards have even worked for small customers of mine to get the attention of mega suppliers. To maximize the impact of the report card, it must be addressed to the head of the company, or at least the head of the site, and it must include a cover letter explaining their performance relative to their past performance and relative to the current performance of competitors or similar suppliers. None of us ever liked bringing home a bad report card. And the head of a company is usually competitive enough that they will not accept a bad report card even if your part of their business is tiny.

Reacting to Supplier Problems

If preventive measures fail, then you need to address supplier problems head-on. This involves first working with them. It may require face-to-face meetings at the highest levels of the organizations where you "take them out to the woodshed" as one of my old bosses used to say. It may require assistance to them from your technical staff. But recognize that it may evolve to where you need to move in a different direction altogether from them.

Communication and SCARs

Suppliers cannot improve their problem areas without good communication from your organization. And the communication must be to a level in the supplier that can (and will) act. Hopefully you established good working relationships when you selected key suppliers whether they supply commodity or custom goods.

Conduct communications with suppliers on problems both verbally and in writing. Email allows knowledge of the issue to be spread out easily. To get across the importance of supply chain issues and the impact you suffer, meet face-to-face – and this does not mean a video call. Yet another reason to keep suppliers close by.

In meeting face-to-face on supplier problems, do not just meet executive to executive. To resolve problems with one supplier that caused us downtime, we sent a van of employees including our union president and two other line workers up to New York to meet with the supplier. The supplier's team included several of their line workers as well. Together we solved a six-month supply problem within two weeks of the meeting – we all got a different perspective from the teams off the floor and both organizations made some changes that improved the floor operation and the supply chain.

Besides written communication in emails, I favor issuing formal Supplier Corrective Action Requests (Figure 6.5) for each incident. And issue them even to sister divisions and to customers that provide the materials.

And when you receive the response to the SCAR from your supplier, do not be afraid to challenge their corrective action if it fails to be preventive. Never accept "we retrained the operators" – not preventive at all!

Help Them Improve Their Performance

A supplier report card system often takes time to change behaviors and performance. You may not be able to wait for that. You may need their improvement now to keep your plant up and operating smoothly.

Supplier Corrective Action Request

Date:	4-Aug	Complaint No.:	0119
Product(s):	Sensitive Teeth Toothpaste	Prod No.:	ST21001
Submitted By:	Jacq Ausen		

Complaint:

Incoming Quality rejected lot F02911 (24,000 tubes) for poor crimps. They found 18/50 bad initially and a re-inspection found 45/125. Some crimps were opened and some popped open with a little pressure placed on the tube. This caused Kitting 2 hours of downtime because they ran out of this product and had to change over production to another product kit.

Supplier:	Acme 2	Supplier Contact:	Mark Louie

To be filled out by the supplier and returned to abcquality@example.xyz within 30 days:

Root Cause of the Problem:

Other Potentially Affected Lots - WIP: _____

Other Potentially Affected Lots - FG: _____

Preventive/
Corrective Action:

On-Site WIP Disposition: _____

On-Site FG Disposition: _____

Notes: _____

Completed By: _____   Date: _____

ABC Quality Review

Received By: _____   Date: _____

Accepted By: _____   Date: _____

Rejected By: Date:

Figure 6.5   Example of Supplier Corrective Action Request form

The first thing to do to help them is to meet face-to-face with them; preferably senior management team to senior management team. Be sure to have some technical or manufacturing representation at this meeting as well – someone who knows the details of the issues. In setting up this meeting, get the supplier's commitment that you will walk away with an improvement plan.

The company may have the resources and skills to address the quality or delivery performance problems themselves. If they do, request a timeline for completion and establish a communications link between the two companies for the improvement effort.

If they do not have the resources and skills, or if you are concerned that they do not, then one way to address this is with a joint engineering team. Send in some of your engineers and manufacturing professionals to work with theirs. This works better with a defined problem that can be attacked in a week-long Kaizen event, but it also works well on problems that can take longer to solve. One thing I also learned is that participation on cross-company teams like this can be a good training ground for young engineers and manufacturing folks.

Another way is to "ask" them to get an outside expert to help. The expertise may need to be in a specific technical field or it might be they need problem-solving expertise to guide their team. I received a call one day from a truck brake manufacturer that I had worked with. They were extensively into lean. The engineer who called me simply said, "Hi Mike, this is Joe O from XYZ. We're having problems with on-time delivery from our label manufacturer. They've shut my cell down twice. I have the owner, Mr. G, here. He needs to speak with you." I started working with Mr. G's team to improve delivery the next week. [Cells and a pull system between companies have worked well.] I have also been hired to work on quality issues as well when companies have had supply chain problems.

Change Suppliers

I have this down near the bottom of the list of ideas to help improve the supply chain when there are quality or delivery issues. It is ahead of "Do it yourself," the next topic, but listed down here because changing suppliers can take a large effort. And many companies have found after a change that there is truth in the old adage "the grass isn't always greener on the other side of the fence." If you do need to change suppliers, follow the same approach as we discussed for selecting good suppliers. Be sure to visit the potential supplier(s) first and audit their systems. Talk to their references. And most of all, make sure that they understand your needs and are totally committed to meeting them for the long term, not committed just long enough to get your business.

Do It Yourself

Years ago, in *In Search of Excellence*, Tom Peters exhorted companies to "Stick to your knitting." In other words, keep producing what you are good at and do not divert attention to other things. But if your suppliers are bad enough, you might need to do just that, make the materials or components you are having problems with.

For most manufacturing companies, making their own packaging would not be sticking to their knitting (unless you are in the packaging supplies business). But one saw blade manufacturer felt compelled to do just that. They had to learn to make packaging supplies to assure the process did not go down for lack of components. On 15 occasions over the prior two years, the company ran out of packs to load their main type of saw blade into. Their main blade line went down on each occasion with the downtime ranging from one hour to two days.

Their suppliers had a myriad of reasons, including snow in New England of all things. They went through three or four packaging suppliers before finally deciding to install their own packaging line with a thermoformer built-in. They had to hire some packaging equipment expertise and fight up the learning curve, but after a few months their supply chain was no longer an issue.

Other companies are doing this as well. Some of the large beverage bottlers are installing blow molders for their plastic bottles – with cost savings and a steady supply. At an aeronautics electronics firm, they started stuffing their own circuit boards after their supply problems led to their major customer threatening to take the business elsewhere. And a chemical company in Delaware started producing their own intermediate chemicals.

Help Set Up a Local Company to Make It

Similarly, to how you could use your team to help improve your existing supplier if their performance is poor, you can use your team to help set up a company to make a raw material or consumable you need.

If possible, work with a local company to do so to minimize the travel distance for your team. A New England materials producer worked with a small resin firm in the region to correct a supply problem they had with a key raw material sourced out of Asia. The regional firm sits four hours away by car instead of 26 hours away by air. The resin firm had never manufactured this type of product, but their equipment and their resin technology knowledge made the new product viable.

Recognize that in addition to providing help from your team, you may also be asked to provide financial support to the project – either in direct funding, in purchasing equipment that you own and they operate, or in a contractual commitment to a minimum purchase quantity.

Leverage Customers

I set this up as the last discussion point on dealing with supplier issues because I hate introducing my customers to my suppliers unless I have to. I hate risking the customer shortening the supply chain by one. But it may come down to needing the leverage of having a big customer behind you to get your supplier to react to your issue. In the few cases one of my teams has done this, we held the meeting in our facility so that we had some control. And we carefully planned out the approach (including pre-meeting conversations with the customer's rep) and set the agenda.

Tough Situations

The toughest situations related to supplier problems arise where:

- Your supplier is another division of your company.
- Your customer defines your supplier.
- Your customer supplies you directly.

These situations make it nearly impossible to change suppliers or do it yourself, but the other approaches discussed in this section remain viable. Communication must be at the forefront – person-to-person, report cards, and SCARs; really no different than for any other supplier.

Unreliable Shipping Companies

Did I tell you about the time the truck with bags of glass fibers went missing and then showed up after hours, unannounced, and three days late with a half-dressed driver, who took out our power gate on the way into our site? It was a trifecta – gate repairs, line downtime, and a late delivery to our main customer!

It does not matter how good a supplier is if you can't get their product. The shipping company is an integral part of your supply chain. Whether you chose the shipper or your supplier does, you need to be certain that you have a reliable one.

My recommendation is that you chose the shipping company for your raw materials unless your supplier is paying for the shipping. And even if you are not paying, you want a say in the shipper. If you are large enough, it is normally advantageous to go with a dedicated shipping company under an annual contract – package your incoming freight with your outgoing. This will help you to get priority in shipping as well as get some added services such as an assigned traffic manager.

If you are a smaller company, try to find a local shipping partner that you can visit face-to-face and establish personal relationships with the employees there. The stronger the relationship that you build, the better service you are going to get for your size.

Some of the areas to consider when selecting a transportation partner include:

- Service coverage in the areas of your key suppliers and in your area.
- Ability to handle full truck loads as well as partials.
- Use of home runs versus terminals. This is especially important with goods that are susceptible to damage in handling (e.g., aluminum can bodies).
- Electronic systems in place for pick-up requests as well as informing you of delivery schedules.
- Do they have their own drivers or are they utilizing subcontractors?
- Are they positioned to provide shipping for your goods as well so that you can leverage incoming and outbound volumes?
- Are they willing to drop trailers at your docks and swap out when empty (or full depending upon goal)?
- What added services can they provide?
- And of course, their cost structure including fuel surcharge rates.

Inconsistent Customer Orders

There have been lots of jokes about customers – "can't live with 'em, can't live without 'em." And customers that are constantly changing orders are among the worst to live with. This is especially true when your biggest customer is all over the map with orders. And it often gets worse the farther down the supply chain you are from the ultimate customer.

But how does your biggest customer pulling in and pushing out orders cause downtime? The most prevalent reason is an increase in changeovers and the downtime associated with those. The best way to take care of changing orders is to get to single-minute changeovers. If you can change over in less than 10 minutes, you have tremendous flexibility in reacting to changes in customers' demands.

However, issues with materials often arise as well – especially when orders are pulled in or are unexpected. It is easy just to say, "Keep some safety stock on hand," especially if this is your biggest customer we are talking about!

Most companies need to hold some safety stocks of critical materials and suppliers – either at their site or at their supplier's. Safety stocks and their levels need active planning and active management by the material management team.

But doesn't it always seem like the safety stock materials you need will be the most expensive or have the longest lead times? You are essentially forced to keep them on hand along with eating the associated cost and risk. Here are a couple of approaches you might try to cut your costs and your risk:

Negotiate with Customers to Keep Long Lead Time Materials on Hand

In the situation where customers order erratically, many companies will be amenable to guaranteeing the use of long-lead time materials within a certain time period. For example, they authorize in writing that they will pay you the full cost for raw materials not used within one year of purchase. You are still out for the cost of the materials until they are used, but there is no risk (okay, I mean lower risk) that you will have to eat that full cost.

Consignment Systems

Getting materials that you hold at your site and then pay for them as they are used is another approach. Certainly, it is better that the supplier holds the safety stock at their facility, but they might not have the space available to do that. Bringing it on-site, but not paying for it until it is consumed, can be a tremendous help to cash flow and mitigate some of the risk for a small company.

At a small thermoset plastic compounding facility, the general manager negotiated a consignment for chopped glass fibers while dealing within a multibillion-dollar industry. He did this by negotiating with a hungrier glass fiber manufacturer, one looking to move into their market. And by trading value – in return for the consignment, the glass fiber manufacturer could use the compounding processes and compounder's laboratory molding equipment for development purposes, the supplier had a win also.

At the end of each month, the compounder mailed a check for the pounds of glass fibers used and provided an inventory report. Once a year, the glass fiber manufacturer sent in an auditor to verify the inventory reports.

Waste Disposal

The backend of the supply chain often gets overlooked – getting rid of waste can also lead to downtime. At a stationery products manufacturer, the guillotine operator was down three or four times per shift hauling the trim cart to a baler completely across the 200,000 sq. ft. plant. Cost – up to 55 minutes per shift of downtime for the guillotine on waste disposal alone.

There are many wastes that build up in processes and that must be removed from the work area – cutting chips, cardboard, pallets, stamping trim, packaging trim, and dust from dust collectors just to name a few. If the operators are doing this and their equipment goes down, then they are not adding any value during that time period.

It may be possible to automate the removal of the waste. The team at the stationery products company came up with two solutions:

- An automated collection system featuring a cutter/blower and a cyclone receiver. Trim would be sucked from the guillotine (and their slitters and sheeters), be chopped up, and be transported via ductwork to a receiver mounted over an automatic compactor/baler.
- Adding a dock section to the building adjacent to the cutting department for locating the baler. The guillotine operator and others would not have to travel across the facility to dump their waste.

This team was able to justify the automation of the trim collection.

Of course, it would be even better to eliminate the waste stream altogether if possible. The suppliers may help with this or you may need some engineering work. In Virginia, one of the box manufacturers went to palletless shipments for its larger customers. The customers needed side grip trucks, not standard fork trucks, to handle these, but for those that used enough boxes, it was worth the investment. The customer we worked with was able to eliminate hundreds of pallets a month coming into the plant and having to be disposed of.

And engineering the waste streams can also eliminate the time needed for waste disposal. At a molding compound facility, we installed a pelletizer that took process fines and re-compacted them. These pellets were recycled back into the product stream. Instead of the process being shut down twice an hour to remove the fines barrel (which was sent to the dump), the process ran continuously. We saved the dump costs and 5–10 minutes of downtime each hour plus we increased throughput by 14% by using the compacted fines.

If you have downtime due to waste disposal, the best approach to tackle it is with a problem-solving team. Their goal should be first to eliminate the waste stream, and if that is not practical, feasible, or cost-effective, then their secondary goal should be to minimize its cost and impact on downtime.

Summary

Working on downtime caused by the supply chain is not as easy as working on set-up reduction or breakdowns. Reducing downtime caused by the supply chain will require partnerships, preventive measures, and systemic changes. And then it will require discipline to keep those in place. Remember these adages – Keep it Close and Keep it Visual.

Chapter 7

Managing the Effort

I'm going to end this book by taking a step backward. We have gone through techniques for reducing process downtime. But how do you know where to focus first, set-up reduction or TPM or one of the other techniques? And how do you know whether you have actually reduced the downtime and are maintaining the gains?

The answer for both of these questions goes back to that famous quote by Rod Tidwell (Cuba Gooding, Jr.) in the film *Jerry Maguire* "Show me the data!" Okay, so he didn't really say that. He shouted the very iconic "Show me the money!" My goal for manufacturers is that "Show me the data!" becomes just as iconic!

You start any improvement effort by collecting the data; you use the data to show what needs to be worked on; and you finish by collecting data to validate that your improvement efforts made real gains and to verify that you are maintaining the gains.

How Much Downtime Do We Have?

Most organizations don't even really know how much downtime they have on their processes, even their critical processes. When I'm touring a factory and I ask the question on downtime, invariably I hear the words "about" and "approximately." When I press the questions further, it becomes evident that the company really doesn't know how much downtime they actually have. And even the companies who appear to be measuring it, usually have

DOI: 10.4324/9781003372714-7

it hidden away in a metric such as OEE where it can be confounded with other measures of operational performance.

Now that is not in all cases. The best plants have reliable numbers for the amount of time that their processes are not operating. They know the "how much" and the "where" – how much downtime they have and from what sources it is coming from. These two points are what workers and management need to know so that they can reduce downtime and then maintain the level achieved. We'll use data collection to get us the "how much" and the "where."

Start Measuring Downtime at the Bottleneck

The place to start measuring downtime is at the bottleneck equipment or process. This is your process step that has the least capacity so it controls production rate of the overall process and maybe even your plant. If you reduce the downtime for this equipment or process step, then you will increase productivity.

Collecting Downtime Data

To know the downtime of the bottleneck (or for any process for that matter), you have to collect the data on all downtime, scheduled or unscheduled. This could be done by the process operators, engineering, or the equipment itself.

The best source of data collection is the last one, when the equipment has sensors built into it and data are automatically collected. Many types of equipment have been set up for the Internet of Things (IoT) or, more lately, IoT 2.0, the Intelligence of Things. Most of these can capture their own performance metrics including downtime.

And even if the equipment or process doesn't have the data capture built-in, simple sensors can be added to capture productivity and downtime data. Using pass-fail relays on the test stand at the end of a balanced assembly line, a team I worked with was able to capture downtime along with productivity and quality. We used a visual display system (Figure 7.1) to drop the relay test performance into a database and to analyze the data in real time. The results were displayed on an overhead dashboard as well as at the assembly line. The only input needed from the operators was the cause of any unplanned downtime.

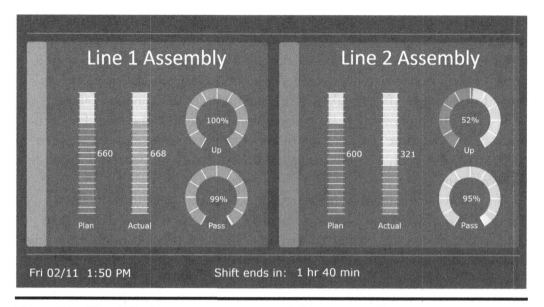

Figure 7.1   Visual display system captures real-time process data

If you can't have the process itself capture the downtime, have a team come in from Engineering or outside the department to collect detailed downtime data so that you can determine where you need to focus your downtime reduction efforts.

At a plastics molding compound supplier, the operations manager combined a look at process downtime with a mass balance to look at yield losses on their most critical process. He assigned process engineers to every shift for two weeks. For those 14 days, the engineers tracked every minute of downtime on all the process equipment and weighed or verified all process inputs and outputs. This included weighing dust removed from dust collectors and even floor sweeping. The engineers used that data to target improvements – after six months, downtime was averaging almost 16% less and yield was up 2.2%, a significant number when you are making millions of pounds a year.

You really don't want the operators to be responsible for capturing the downtime data at least in the early phases of the data collection. You can have them help by identifying causes, but try not to have them actually record the minutes or hours down (of course, if you have to, you have to).

The reasons for this are twofold. First, having the operators collect downtime data takes away from what they should be doing – adding value by making product! And second, you don't always get accurate downtime measurements, sometimes intentionally. At one company, my audit of operator-collected data found that the break time that averaged 15.0 minutes with a range of 0 on paper actually averaged 24.5 minutes from last piece before break to first piece after break. There was a little point shaving going on!

If using an engineering team or operators to record the reason for each instance of downtime, create a list of the downtime codes that they are to use. Don't leave it up to them to decide on how to write out the reason for the downtime.

Once you have a form or approach, be certain to train those collecting the data on what the issues are behind each reason code. Train them also how to assign the proper code. For example, a process might be going down for a product changeover, but the need for the changeover was driven by a key raw material not being on hand. The root cause of the downtime is the raw material availability, not the product changeover itself.

Whether you have an outside team come in to collect the data or the operators do it, don't just have them keep a log. It used to be that you'd

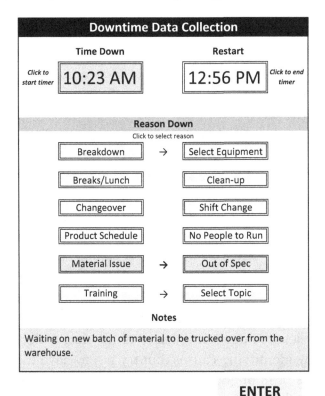

Figure 7.2   Downtime data collection form

create a paper form and manually capture the data. Today you can employ electronics to make it easier and faster. It can be a pdf form created for a tablet or laptop computer that aggregates the data into a spreadsheet format (Figure 7.2). Or a bar code system where the operator or engineer scans a reason code (Figure 7.3) and the time and reason gets sent to a database.

Downtime Reason Codes

Scan the reason code to start the downtime timer

	Loading Material		Clean-Up		No Operator
	Lunch/Breaks		Adjusting Process		Team Activities
	Set-Up		1st Piece Inspection		Quality Issue
	Preventive Maintenance		No Material		Training
	Breakdown		Nothing Scheduled		Other
Scan Run when the process is ready to operate again.					
			Run		

Figure 7.3   QR codes for downtime reasons

When the period of downtime ends, a "Run" code is scanned so the system brackets the time period when the equipment wasn't running.

Can you use paper and pencil to capture the downtime? Certainly! Industry did that for decades. Our grandparents did that and then analyzed the data with slide rule calculations. It can be done, but that's not efficient these days.

Regardless of your approach, ensure that all sources of downtime are considered and then make it easy to collect the data.

Even when using bar codes or QR codes instead of a manual form, if you are relying on operators and engineers, i.e., people, to record the downtime, you face the risk of incomplete or erroneous data. You are better off setting up measurement equipment to catch the downtime automatically.

Identifying the Vital Few

Once we have the data, we need to analyze it. We look for the sources of downtime that cause the most pain – those that stop our equipment from running for the greatest number of hours.

- Look at how many downtime hours stem from each source.
- Identify the downtime costs due to each source.
  - Unscheduled downtime typically has more costs associated with it.

We'll apply the Pareto Principle to identify where to attack the downtime first.

Pareto Diagrams

The Pareto Principle, or the 80-20 rule as quality guru Joseph Juran coined it, is derived from the work of the 19th-century Italian economist Vilfredo Pareto. He observed that the majority of wealth (i.e., land, at the time) was in the hands of a small number of citizens. Juran expanded upon this to quality and manufacturing saying that in most cases the majority of the effects on an issue are from only a few of the causes. Those few causes are the "vital few" and all of the others are the "trivial many." This will be true with your downtime causes as well. Most of the downtime will only come from a few of the causes. To reduce the downtime most effectively, you must first start by focusing on those vital few causes.

The vital few can be shown graphically with a Pareto diagram (Figure 7.4). Here, the contributions of the downtime causes are bars plotted in descending order against the left-hand y-axis. The cumulative percentage line is plotted on the right-hand y-axis. With a Pareto diagram, it is easy to see where to focus the downtime improvement efforts.

For the company whose data are shown in Figure 7.4, the first three causes, missing fasteners, air leaks, and electronics issues, contribute to over 80% of the downtime. These should be attacked first because the efforts there will have the greatest impact on the operation.

Attack the Downtime

Using the techniques from this book, you are going to work to reduce the downtime starting with the top source of downtime. For our example, you would start by forming a problem-solving team to look at the root causes of why fasteners are missing. When that team completes its task, another team can be formed to work on air leaks, then on to the electronics. You just work your way down the list, eventually to where you break up the current "Other" category to work on the downtime issues making up that category.

As you work down the list, you may "pass" the improved level of downtime for one of the causes already worked on. For example, let's say that the team on fasteners missing reduced that downtime from 15 hours per

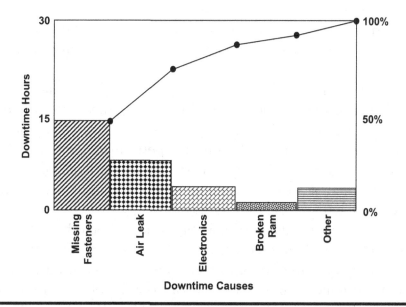

Figure 7.4   Pareto diagram of downtime causes

month to seven hours per month. After working on air leaks, we could have another team look at missing fasteners to see if we can reduce below the 7-hour level before we move on to work on the electronics issues.

Monitor Downtime Going Forward

Who Should Measure Downtime Long-Term?

Even if you use an outside team to capture the downtime and collect detailed data initially to determine where you need to take action, you want the person or team responsible for the process to monitor and report the downtime in the long run. Having them measure it and report it gives them ownership. And measuring it will help ensure that whatever gains you made with downtime reduction are maintained.

Run Charts

To show downtime over time, the best tool to use is a run chart (Figure 7.5) – with time on the x-axis and downtime in hours on the y-axis.

Keep All Eyes on the Target

Most organizations record the downtime for each process on a daily basis. The run charts can be used to quickly identify any unusual downtime levels and any adverse trends. They should be posted daily on the dashboard for each process.

The downtime run chart should be a key feature in the daily Tier 1 (supervisor/team leader and operators) shift start-up meeting at the dashboard as shown in Figure 7.6. Operators should be trained to point out unusual downtime performance (or unusual performance for any of the KPIs) from the day before. The supervisor/team leader would escalate any abnormal downtime or adverse trends up to the manager level in the daily Tier 2 meeting.

While the operators and supervisor/team leader should be held responsible for downtime including measuring and reporting it, management must be the ones to monitor the performance. If management never looks at the downtime measurements and reports, it will soon be obvious to those taking the measurements that what they are doing is not important. The measurements will soon go away and downtime will creep back up.

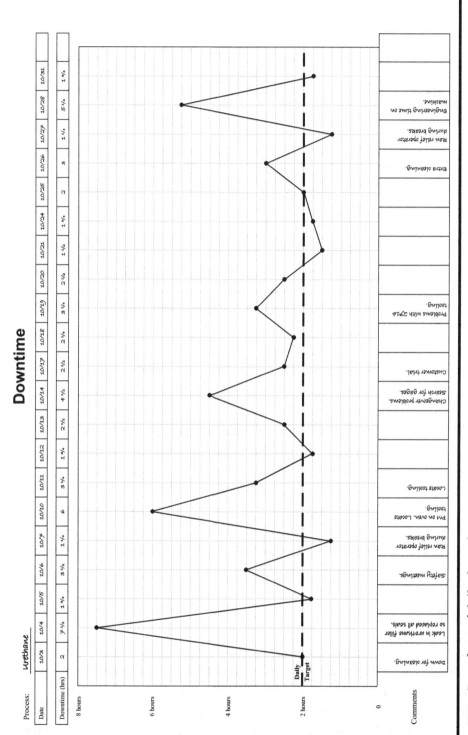

Figure 7.5 Run chart of daily downtime

Figure 7.6   Review downtime daily at Tier 1 shift start-up meeting. *Photo courtesy of Horst Engineering.*

Managers should cover downtime performance for key processes on exception basis (i.e., only discuss if there is change in downtime performance) at the weekly or monthly Tier 3 meetings of the site executive team and the managers. But this alone doesn't transfer the importance out to the floor. The site executive team and the managers should review downtime and other KPI metrics on their daily walks around the facility. And "review" includes asking questions of the operators and recognizing good performances.

Management monitoring downtime also ensures that overemphasis on downtime does not lead to bad side effects such as quality or line speed (performance) dropping off. This can often be accounted for by the management team monitoring a balanced scorecard.

Balanced Scorecard

This book is on downtime reduction, but just looking at downtime in a vacuum can create other problems. I've seen workforces that focused so much on downtime and "productivity" that their quality dropped off significantly. And in others I've seen a change to longer runs to minimize downtime from product changeovers. This impacted their on-time delivery and their flexibility – more than a few customers became very frustrated with the longer lead times and late orders.

These anecdotes show why the concept of a balanced scorecard remains so important. A balanced scorecard helps managers ensure their improvement gains in one area are not being offset by losses in other areas.

Typical key performance indicators (KPIs) cover:

- Safety
- Quality
- Delivery
- Productivity
- Cost

An organization needs to ensure that all of these are trending in the right direction – Cost and Safety (number of accidents) going down; Quality, Delivery, and Productivity going up.

Downtime can be used separately as a KPI but commonly makes up part of the Productivity metric in the form of Overall Equipment Effectiveness (OEE).

OEE

OEE helps answer the question "Did we get the maximum amount of good product out today for the time we planned the process to run?" Breaking that sentence down, OEE has three components: Availability, Performance, and Quality.

OEE is the product of these three as a percentage:

$$OEE = A \times P \times Q \times 100\%$$

Availability (A): this metric is the fraction of the planned production time that the process or equipment operates.

$$A = \frac{\text{Planned Production Time} - \text{Downtime}}{\text{Planned Production Time}}$$

Planned Production Time in the Availability calculation takes the total work time for the shift or day and subtracts out breaks, lunch, meetings, and staffing reallocations.

I do not like this definition. To me, Availability on the bottleneck operation should be calculated on the time the equipment could be available to make a product – the entire shift for a one-shift operation and 24 hours for a three-shift operation – not the Planned Production Time. I'd have none of this subtracting time out for breaks and lunch or for when we're not scheduling the line because we don't have the people to staff it. This would also prevent gamesmanship on what Planned Production Time is. We need all the uptime possible on our bottleneck operations.

Performance (P): the fraction of the ideal speed that the process or equipment runs at.

$$P = \frac{\text{Units Made}/\text{Time}}{\text{Ideal Speed in Units}/\text{Time}}$$

Performance is how many units of product did we make in a given run time versus how many units should we have made if we had been running the equipment at its design or ideal speed during that entire time. Performance is not a comparison with production standards. Most companies create production standards that are levels reduced from either the design speed or ideal speed of the equipment. The reason for incorporating ideal speed is that if you use Design of Experiments or another improvement method to increase the design speed, then this new level should become part of the Performance metric. At a canning operation in Virginia, we took a 120 can per minute (cpm) filler-seamer and figured out how to increase its speed to 150 cpm. 150 cpm became the denominator in their Performance calculation going forward.

Quality (Q): the fraction of good units produced by the process or equipment.

$$Q = \frac{\text{Total Units Made} - \text{Rejected Units}}{\text{Total Units Made}}$$

Quality is straightforward, but care should be taken not to take a "double hit" for quality issues. In a powder packaging line I worked with, unsealed bags were counted as rejected units. Once enough were accumulated, these were fed back into the mixer and repackaged with the time for this rework being counted as downtime. Here the team got penalized in both the Quality metric as well as the Availability metric.

Keep Learning

Now you understand some basic downtime reduction techniques and have some ideas on how to determine where to put your efforts and how to monitor your successes. But your journey is not over here. I'm a great fan of learning – I even recently took a great MOOC online entitled *Learning How to Learn* with Dr. Barbara Oakley (an EE by the way) and Dr. Terrence Sejnowski. The techniques in this book may be your starting point for knowledge on reducing downtime or may just reinforce things you already knew. Either way, I challenge you – to challenge yourself and your team to keep learning and applying that learning to continue the effort to reduce your downtime to zero! Let me know how you make out.

Glossary of Acronyms

5Ss: sort, set-in-order, shine, standardize, and sustain

8-D: eight-discipline [problem-solving model]

AI: artificial intelligence

APICS: formerly the American Production and Inventory Control Society

ARIMA: autoregressive integrated moving average [chart]

CMM: coordinate measuring machine

CMMS: computerized maintenance management system

CNC: computer-numerical control, used in this text to refer to CNC machining centers

DOE: design of experiments

EDI: electronic data interchange [between companies]

ERP: enterprise resource planning [computer system]

EWMA: exponentially weighted moving average [chart]

FEA: finite element analysis

FMEA: failure mode and effects analysis

GIGO: garbage in - garbage out

GP: general purpose

HAZOP: hazards and operability study

KPI: key performance indicator

MOQ: minimum order quantity

OEE: overall equipment effectiveness

PdM: predictive maintenance

PLC: programmable logic controller

PM: preventive maintenance

ROI: return on investment

SCAR: supplier corrective action request
SKU: stock-keeping unit
SMED: single minute exchange of die
TPM: total productive maintenance
WIP: work-in-process [inventory], aka waste-in-process if there is excess

Glossary of Terms

Balanced activities: ensuring that task times are balanced between team members working on a set-up or preventive maintenance or other activity so that no team member becomes idle waiting for another to complete their tasks.

Balanced scorecard: balancing your KPIs so that improvement efforts in one area aren't made at the expense of a drop-off in another area of a company's performance.

Cross-training: having workers trained in each other's tasks so they can provide back-up if someone is absent.

External time: the time during the set-up that the activities are performed while the equipment operates making saleable product.

Internal time: the time during the set-up that activities are performed with the process down.

Kanban: a signal that more material needs to be produced or obtained. This can be in the form of a card or in the form of an empty space.

Poka Yoke: mistake-proofing, with the goal of preventing errors or mistakes.

SMED: single-minute exchange of die, or more generally, set-ups that take less than 10 minutes.

Total productive maintenance: an overall approach to maintenance involving the operators, maintenance, and engineering applying preventive maintenance, preventive engineering, and predictive maintenance technique to prevent breakdowns.

Index

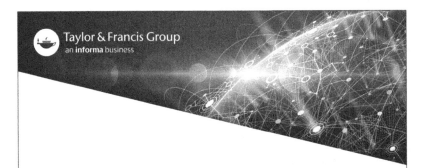